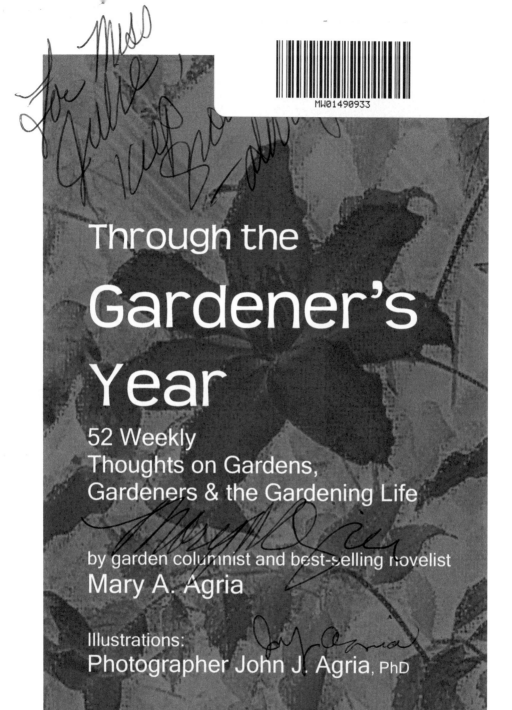

Through the
Gardener's
Year

52 Weekly
Thoughts on Gardens,
Gardeners & the Gardening Life

by garden columnist and best-selling novelist
Mary A. Agria

Illustrations:
Photographer John J. Agria, PhD

Revised and edited from columns originally published
in the Petoskey News-Review, Mi • 2007-2014

Clematis

Thanks goes to Babette Stenuis of the *Petoskey News-Review* for first proposing these columns back in 2006; to Debbie McGuiness and the editors who kept it going, and to my spouse and agent, John, for his never-failing support and inspiration. His photographs capture in subtle black and white, the heart and spirit the gardener's vision. Special thanks to Ellen McGill for her faithful and wise editing and input. And finally, I give thanks to and for my Mom, Lydia, a much loved and influential 'master gardener' in my life. Without her values and wisdom, this book would not have been possible.

visit Mary Agria online at www.maryagria.com
for excerpts from her work, for special features and to arrange
for live or online author chats, signings or book talks.
Available in bookstores and from online booksellers, from
Lulu.com, and in some cases, in Kindle format.

— Through the Gardener's Year —

We all do battle with unseasonable dry spells over the years. To survive—even grow—beyond those difficult droughts of the soul, we learn to root out our share of quack grass, turn over spadefuls of spent or decimated ground and plant again. Though we may not call ourselves gardeners, it is the human experience.

From Time in a Garden, Mary Agria, 2006

On Time and the Garden

Like the heroine of my Life in the Garden novels, Eve Brennerman, I became a garden columnist late in life. It is not the kind of career path anyone commonly chooses on high school career days. The journey to this place and time in my life story had its share of detours. But after moving from climate zone to climate zone across the U.S. and gardening throughout all of my adult life, there is a certain inevitability or at least logic about where I find myself.

At the heart of my personal and the gardener's journey is an unfolding encounter with time, the seasons and what they mean in the human experience. In Western culture, time often is perceived as a linear concept and process. Some might describe it as the forward march of history. Awareness of humankind's journey begins with the roaming prehistoric hunter-gatherers and Stone Age dawn of civilization. At some point along the continuum, one of our early nomadic ancestors discovered that if a seed is stuck in the ground, a crop will grow in the season that follows. That first ancestral farmer made a compact with the earth. If the plant and earth are tended, both will respond.

History catalogs innovation upon innovation that shapes life as we know it: from flint points to high-tech digital discoveries yet to transform the planet. The past gives way to what is built upon that past, namely the future. The present—the now—is valued first and foremost for its transformative potential. And so, over time, the contributions of the early gardeners with their digging sticks have led modern agriculture to mechanized plows, planters and harvesters manipulated by remote control from the farmer's living room like some space age video game. Even the culture of 'the land' is driven by the entrepreneurial.

And yet for many religious traditions, as well as cultures in other parts of the world, time and human history is viewed in a very different light. Time for many spiritual traditions is cyclical—not just an ever forward-moving stream. The inner human experience unfolds as a seasonal quest for ever deeper encounters with the Holy. Year after year, ancient liturgical traditions, lectionaries, recurring feasts, festivals and calendars lend precious structure to the shared faith journey of the world's religious communities. Time becomes a perpetual search for truths held sacred and eternal, the meaning behind humanity's story. Ever changing. Ever changeless.

Christians call this liturgical structure *Seasons of the Church Year*. The Judaic experience from which the Christian tradition derives its underlying belief system celebrates its own unique seasonal heritage through thousands of years, far removed physically in time and place from the original historic events, yet as immediate as the Now.

And so it is with time in a garden. Gardeners intuitively understand and share such a cyclical view of time. The gardening life orients itself around seasons that reappear year after year. 'New Years' may come and go. But in a sense, time stands still within the gardening season's circle-round—becomes common ground with which gardeners everywhere can identify. Come flood, come drought, come brutal cold and untimely thaws, time in the garden provides a spiritual connection to generations of plants and gardeners, past and future. Seedtime and harvest sustain not just humanity's physical existence and survival, but our very deepest emotional and spiritual needs. It is no accident that gardening remains the most popular 'hobby' even in our technology-obsessed world. On a spiritual level, gardening 'grounds' us.

Gardening has power to shape not just land but lives. In a control-obsessed world, gardens and gardeners battle forces that forever elude and challenge, the vagaries of wind and sleet and blistering sun. Quickly as they pursue their craft, gardeners as children of the earth learn to look inward to make sense of that struggle with the paradoxes of existence. Life emerges from the soil, dust to which ultimately all return. Transience and the Eternal become inseparable.

Perhaps this is why die-hard gardeners often love to read about their art. In the Life in the Garden novels, Eve Brennerman uses an undated Gardener's Calendar of Quotations every year to ground her and order her days. Now and then she shuffles the dog-eared quote-a-day deck and begins again. It is in that same spirit that 52 essays in this book are organized and selected. Together they take the reader week by week through the seasons. But taken independently, each in its own way explores what makes gardeners and gardens grow.

With gratitude I dedicate this book to all the gardeners who have helped shape my love of green things growing. And I give thanks for the many gardens in my life, from the Midwest to New England and the American Southwest. They have been the very best teachers of all.

Mary A. Agria
Petoskey, Michigan • Tempe, Arizona

January

A fresh snowfall—winter's mulch—protects the slumbering, frozen Northern Michigan landscape.

AT THE TURNING OF THE YEAR
First published in January, 2012

A New Year has begun. The feared Mayan Apocalypse fizzled. Snowbirds fly south. Skiers wing their way north. A gardener quietly dreams of the growing season to come, a quest that drives us all our lives.

As a landmark for marking ends and beginnings, New Year celebrations are no simple business. I spent that night in childhood feasting on pickled herring and cheese curds, the custom from my German-American roots. At dusk, my brother and I would start a jigsaw puzzle, our goal to finish by midnight. We chose a harder one every year.

When my husband was a boy, he was convinced that if something awesome or awful was about to happen, it was bound to be at that fateful stroke of midnight. Then came television, with not just *one* New Year celebration, but *many*, hour after hour across the country and even the globe. A young boy's world view changed literally overnight.

Resetting the Clock

Some years ago, headed west in our motorhome to spend the year-end holidays with family, my spouse and I had another life-shaping encounter with time. At home in wintery New England, fall was long-since past. But as we racked up the miles through Virginia, then the Carolinas and Georgia, we were struck by a strange sense of deja vu. Barren tree limbs along the parkway subtly transformed themselves into brilliant leafy forests of reds and golds and oranges. In the short space of 48 hours, we left winter behind and relived autumn in all its glory.

Not just time was out of joint. I could have sworn those trees were oaks, but the colors resembled northern maples. It was my first brush with the Southern Live Oak. Actually an evergreen, it can live upwards of a millennium. Despite multiple hurricanes in a single season, University of Southern Mississippi's Friendship Oak has hit the ripe old age of 500.

That wonderful snowbird journey became an enduring wake-up call for the psyche. New Year is not just about champagne and funny hats. It is meant to help us make sense of time. Like our ancient agrarian ancestors, we modern children of the earth depend on seasonal milestones to govern the rhythm of our lives. Amid our culture of control freaks and obsession with certitude, we gardeners still wrestle with truths that matter for humanity's physical, emotional and spiritual survival.

Try as we might to predict the future, change is a fundamental fact of life. And gardens teach us to cope with it better than anything I know.

Shadows of Things to Come

Window: Church of the Redeemer, Mattituck, New York

First published February, 2010

Poet T. S. Eliot called April "the cruellest month". But a British researcher, Dr. Cliff Arnall of Cardiff University, claims the most depressing season actually comes in mid-January. Holiday trimmings are gone. Bills are piling up. Our New Year resolve is waning. And yet, hope springs. Blooming in a quiet sanctuary, hidden among the dry stalks of winter, lilies of the valley grow—harbingers of eternal spring.

SOUL SEARCHING
First published in January, 2013

Winter invites reflection, especially for gardeners in northern climes who brave bone-chilling cold for any signs of life. Patience comes hard. But while our gardens sleep under two feet of snow, we gain precious perspective. In the process, we learn a great deal about ourselves.

No two gardeners (or gardens) are alike. Some prefer annuals. Results are instantaneous. Personally, I love perennials—old friends that stick with me season after season. And if something is growing, I leave it. As plants crowd to fill the vacant territory between them, I wait as long as possible to intervene. Rather than garden stakes to maintain order, I turn to strong-stalked plants to shore up their more fragile neighbors.

Invasive species have a distinct advantage with my gardening style. If I am not careful, I wind up with an unruly bed full of tough plants like Siberian iris, with roots so thick that it takes a machete or back-hoe to keep them from taking over. "Kind surgeons leave stinking wounds," the old Dutch proverb urges. Finally, after 15 years of my live-and-let-live style, my husband had to intervene. He hired a crew to help me get the beds under control again.

A game changer was to work one summer on a community garden team, led by a 'bare earth' gardener, hell-bent on structure and keeping a good bit of open ground between the plants. *OCD. Obsessive Compulsive Disorder*, I sniffed. And then right off, I drew the job of rooting out a perfectly good patch of succulents that had crept into the lilies. It was tempting to rebel. But by summer's end, I had found a new-found respect for ways to keep a plant community co-existing peacefully.

The Southwest is no stranger to this clash of gardening styles. The instinct is to let things go here. Life struggles so hard to survive in a desert. With irrigation, bushes can flower wildly year-round. But local landscapers are notorious for hacking back bougainvillea and oleander, even when in full flower. In the blink of an eye, the showy plants are reduced to flowerless green mounds.

A trifle sad, I decided. True, discipline and order have their place. Plants can thrive on it. But then there is something to be said for spontaneity, creativity, growth. Everything deserves its chance to flower.

Here's to finding that hard middle ground—the balance—in the things we nurture. As gardeners. As parents or grandparents. As teachers. neighbors and public officials. Not a bad resolution for any New Year.

For everything its season. Snow still blankets the East and Upper Midwest. Meanwhile new life bursts forth in dramatic fashion in the Desert Botanical Garden, Phoenix, Arizona.

RESOLUTIONS
First published in January, 2008

Up north, my summer garden slumbers under its coverlet of white. Meanwhile I sit idly at my computer, contemplating how to make my time as a gardener more productive and meaningful in the coming year:

Tackle the Tough Stuff Early: At the risk of rooting out an occasional perennial by mistake, every hour I spend going after those pesky weeds at first sight can save days of misery later on when the roots are more firmly established. So, the minute that frost is out of the ground, *go get 'em!*

Dare to Experiment: Nursery catalogs have begun to arrive. As I pour over the glossy and exotic photos, I find myself itching to stray off the path of the tried and true. What's the worst that could happen if I risk cultivating that unfamiliar beauty? Go for it!

Know When to Fold: For years I've been trying to make my front yard garden into a carpet of sunny blooms. Problem? Deep shade. It's time to give it up—dig in ferns and hostas, and for color, invest in flowering annuals that thrive in black-hole-of-Calcutta conditions. To reward myself for that reality check, this summer I vow to expand the backyard beds for all those great prairie plants that demand full sun to thrive. The nice thing about plants: they don't say, "I told you so."

Cultivate Whimsy: Much as I admire gardeners who populate their plots with solid masses of color, I cannot seem to force myself to root out the "strays". The great stained glass artist Louis Comfort Tiffany deliberately set a flawed piece of glass into each of his magnificent windows. Perfection, he said, is for heaven. May I acquire the grace to appreciate the spontaneous in my garden for what it is: a gift.

Stop and Smell the Roses: Like many folks with day jobs, gardening for me was often something I fitted in along the fringes of my life. On the way to the car, I bent to pull a few weeds. Carrying out the trash, I propped up a few stems of wind-bent iris. This year, I also will spend more time just *enjoying.* Coffee in hand, I'll start the day strolling my pocket gardens when the dew still glistens on the leaves. Tired or not, at sunset I'll make the time to watch the flower petals curling in on themselves for the night.

All gardeners, spoken or unspoken, make a compact with the earth, year in and year out. The garden's job is to grow. The gardener's is to nurture, and yes, ***appreciate***. Sounds suspiciously like life to me.

Appearances can deceive. Exotic looking Passion Flowers were not indigenous (or likely survivors) in the climate zone of the author's New York garden. But these 'annuals' naturalized anyway—go figure !

ROSES IN THE SNOW
First published in 2010

It is an understatement to say that a second winter has arrived in the East and Upper Midwest. The word is slammed—snow, sleet, freezing rain and everything in between. The crooners on the radio pleading for a white Christmas last November seem to have gotten a little carried away.

For a gardener, these are worrisome times. We fret over what may be happening to those plants of ours out there alone in the dark. And when it comes to keeping our own spirits up, half-priced and drooping poinsettias in the supermarket can't quite cut it. Poinsettias have been described as the most abused house plants, *ever*. Chances of their survival into the New Year are slim to none. And the local greenhouse has closed for the season to save energy costs. We can't even walk the aisles, taking in the reassuring scent of warm earth and chlorophyll.

Winter becomes the ultimate test of a gardener's character. How resilient are we in the winter 'down times'? We know how much damage those relentless winds and blizzards can do. A garden can fall victim to a longed-for thaw as well as a hard freeze. Patience and wisdom are called for in large doses. That, and hope.

The gardener's dilemma is pretty much 'ripped from the headlines'. No one quite trusts that the better-than-anticipated holiday retail season guarantees an economy in recovery. The tourism business agonizes over weather forecasts. The unemployed struggle.

Samuel Johnson described second marriages as the "triumph of hope over experience", a thought Anne Bronte also borrows in her wonderful novel, *Tenant of Wildfell Hall*. We gardeners cannot predict what our acres and furrows will look like in three months. We can only trust our own persistence as we confront what lies ahead.

My rallying cry to gardeners everywhere is, "Take heart!" In all the changes of our changing times, some things never change:

—How we treat our garden impacts the earth beyond us.

—Plants we share can enrich the lives of others.

—What we sow, we may not always reap. But if we do not take a chance and plant, nothing can grow. *Keep a green tree in your heart*, a Chinese proverb says, *and a singing bird might come.*

And history indeed repeats itself. The most commonly recorded New Year's resolution in ancient Babylon was to return borrowed garden tools.

14

Roses in bloom in January? In Northern Michigan, not quite. But greeting the new year, hens-and-chicks brave the morning chill at a historic mission along California's Camino Real. How we define winter, cold and the turning of the seasons all boils down to location, location, location.

AWAKE, O WINTERY EARTH
First published in January, 2009

I love the composer J. S. Bach's classic celebration of the season, "Awake, O Wintery Earth". The subtle rhythm of his music is perfect for the poetry of the text, images of the winter garden, rousing itself from its slumbers. But for a garden to come alive, for perennial plants to survive that dark season, a gardener needs to think ahead.

Every fall, perennials need help to acclimatize or 'harden' themselves to face the lack of sunlight and brutal cold to come. Many hibernate, storing up nutrients in their underground tubers or tap roots, to provide sustenance for the barren winter months. Plants that are nutritionally 'balanced' are most likely to survive.

Wise gardeners should stop using fertilizer six weeks before the normal first frost date and avoid slow-release nutrients late in the season. Spiking levels of nitrogen too late in fall can stimulate new growth that will make plants vulnerable to severe winter conditions.

Watering patterns in the growing season also impact the hardiness of perennials. To keep September rains from producing an untimely growth spurt, adequate summer watering is needed that enables fertilizers to be absorbed into the plant structure, well before first frost. If faced with fall drought conditions or under-watering, root storage decreases. Plants do not absorb enough energy to grow new shoots in spring.

Mid-winter thaws may be wonderful for morale, but such unseasonable warm spells can be hard on plants. Sustained warm weather, before its time, undermines the hardiness of many plants. Intense, untimely sunlight on frost-covered evergreens can lead to freeze or 'burn' damage. Foliage may or may not return to normal once spring growth begins. The drying effect of wind can be equally harmful. Savvy gardeners can resort to mulch or 'blankets' to protect plants against such harsh winter conditions.

Life lessons abound here for our own personal journeys. How richly and fully we live impacts not just the here and now, but the future. Shallow roots can be dangerous. Careful cultivation of inner resources becomes a strong hedge against the tougher times that are bound to come.

Gardening and the gardener's life are acquired skills. The art of keeping hope alive, under even the bleakest of conditions, is not for the faint of heart. It takes not just hard work, but wise and careful preparation.

16

February

The joy of new life emerging is a theme in the author's
Second Leaves: Growing Young Gardeners **(2012).**

MEMORY THERAPY
First published in January, 2009

The January thaw is history. Temperatures and wind chills are falling to unprecedented lows. Only thoughts of green things growing can sustain my inner gardener. The rush of holiday mail was a brief distraction from the gales. Then yesterday, a plant catalog arrived, a precious glimpse of what is possible once that final melt-down signals the coming of spring.

For the gardener who seemingly has everything, plant-of-the-month memberships can be an intriguing gift: a way year-round to satisfy that powerful urge to watch things grow and flourish. Another favorite winter pick-me-up is an impromptu field trip to the local florist. Or simply stand dead still in floral department of the local supermarket, close your eyes and draw in the heady 'green' smell of plants about to bloom. For a split-second, the graying mounds of snow outside become a distant memory.

Venturing farther afield to the nearest greenhouse or garden show-- priceless. The first glass and cast iron ribbed 'winter garden' appeared at the British World Fair of 1848, the brainchild of Sir Joseph Paxton. The man should get a medal for his contribution to mental health. Plants heal. Though his Crystal Palace later was destroyed by fire, its imitators live on as pilgrimage sites for winter-weary tourists around the world.

As I write, on the East Coast, a record monster storm is burying mega-cities in mountains of white. Amid nostalgic talk of Ice Bowls and record cold, even die-hard NFL fans are tempted to skip the playoffs and stay home. The darkness of winter nights seems interminable.

Grounds for despair? At heart, we gardener folk know better. Memories know no season. Fresh as yesterday, lily-of-the-valley wafts subtly from the bottle of my Wisconsin grandmother's favorite perfume. I kept it for years on my dresser. In a faded photo, a purple cloud of wisteria floats over the gate of my beloved New York garden. Under a thick sheet of white along the Michigan shore line, I can almost hear the Memorial Garden's hellebores unfurling their leaves to the sun.

Spring to the gardener is not just a season. It is a state of mind. Gardening teaches the human spirit to cultivate a sense of expectation that defies sub-zero forecasts and driveways sheathed in treacherous black ice. The garden that lives on in our wintery imaginations becomes a passport to a kinder, gentler time that lies ahead.

Hope lives again where only barren ground has been. Some years we just need to work harder to believe it than others.

18

Fierce and determined, crocus shivers through a late winter snow in the author's Long Island, New York garden.

CULTIVATING PATIENCE

First published in February, 2013

Some pundits have described ours as a nation in which instant gratification rules. Kids are labeled undisciplined. Far too many so-called citizens avoid sacrifice at all costs. The best antidote I know for such we-want-it-now value systems is to walk the garden in the winter.

A reality check began months ago, with the annual fall garden take-down. Gardeners often take the process hard. It hurts to see beloved perennials reduced to dry, stubbly stalks and root mounds. But gardeners also know that the future depends on such tough love.

Winter snows bury the evidence of all that purposeful destruction, shroud the bare earth in a dazzling sheet of white. It is a time of healing. For under that protective, insulating coverlet, the sleeping garden begins to recoup its losses. Let the howling winds do their worst, the garden has begun to repair and prepare itself to grow and bloom again.

We walk the winter garden as a spiritual exercise. Our senses strain to spot signs of better things to come. We learn to scale our expectations to celebrate the tiniest of green shoots around the base of a thawing downspout. Faint footprints in the snow mark our journey.

Don't want too much too soon, we caution. Rushing the spring season can have dire consequences for a plant or flower bed. Time must unfold in a rhythm beyond our control. Humbling, we realize, but honest.

Those who experience winter in the Southwest for the first time may believe that there is no turn of the seasons as Midwesterners know it. They quickly discover they are mistaken. The briefest of killing frosts sends the leaves cascading down. Change may be subtler than a lake-effect storm roaring across Michigan's Little Traverse Bay. But the signs of change are there, if we attune ourselves to see them.

Nothing stays the same. Rarely are the things worth having born in an instant. The winter garden teaches us to watch for and appreciate what time can accomplish. In just a few short months, an explosion of green will make that long, dark winter fade in our memories. In the meantime, expectation becomes a life-transforming force, like sap rising in the sturdy trunk of the maple or the gnarled and aged grapevines as they strain toward bud break.

A good thing, this business of learning to wait. Life-renewing power is unleashed as we sense hope slowly build within us. Our gardens thrive on that patient unfolding. So do we.

An elegant columbine in bloom in the desert? There It
was, flowering in the Arizona spring wildflower exhibit
at the Phoenix Botanical Garden. At their best, gardens
challenge and teach us to rethink the possible.

GARDENING 101
First published in January, 2010

A recent product recall by "Baby Einstein" concedes that plunking young children in front of the TV is not a guarantee of greater intelligence or mental health. Workout fads come and go. Gardening can accomplish many of the same things with a lot smaller outlay of cash.

A U.K. National Trust survey says that more than 70 percent of Britains—renowned as a 'Nation of Gardeners'—believe spending time in a garden is vital for a healthy quality of life. Digging in beds and tending plants can have a positive impact on self-esteem. It even improves a person's love life. Four out of five British believe schools ought to teach children about gardening and growing plants.

Right now, many gardens lie frozen and dormant. That doesn't keep us from tweaking our Bucket List for the growing season to come:

Get Outside—outside the box, the house, our personal boundaries that limit growth. Dare to risk. If you can't bring yourself to plant a garden, *transplant.* Prepare to move a houseplant outdoors for summer vacation. When I took one with me on a book tour last year, it proved an amazing experience for me. The plant has never been happier.

Keep Growing. I would be the first to admit my technical knowledge of soils is pitiful. No excuses. I need to do whatever it takes to *learn.* Plants are born to grow. So are we. It's how life works.

Connect. Gardens cut across the generations. Grandchildren's visits becomes an opportunity to grow another gardener. Plant *their* special bush together, then teach them how to care for it. My youngest daughter invited me to celebrate her New Year birthday together one year by volunteering at a local Urban Garden project. I was surprised and thrilled. She doesn't even own a house plant and her yard is a disaster.

Lighten Up. We are an Obsessive Compulsive nation. When I taught third graders, their favorite story was *Ferdinand the Bull*—the classic tale of a fierce-looking young bull who just wanted to sit under a cork tree and smell the roses. Boys in that class were the ones who 'got it' the most. Resist turning gardening into a competition. My tomato doesn't have to be bigger than yours to taste great. I don't need to grow the most zucchini in the neighborhood. Beauty is its own reward. The thrill of budding and sprouting and flowering needs no blue ribbon.

Spring is coming. Days are getting longer. Time to sharpen hoes and clippers, arming us for another summer in the garden's life.

Primrose glisten in the melting snow of the author's
garden, Long Island, New York.

ICE AGE REVISITED

First published in January, 2007

The memorial garden in Michigan where I volunteer every summer has a web-cam now, year-round, mounted a phone pole. Half a continent away in sunny Arizona, in the dead of winter, I find myself fretting over images online of those precious acres.

Michigan's lack of snow, followed by rounds of freezing and thawing, can wipe out our daisies in a heartbeat. To grow or not to grow? With temperatures spiking and dipping, the poor plants haven't a clue. Climate maps for the Upper Midwest show Zone 5-6, so the perennials chosen by our garden team should be able to survive low-end temperatures ranging from −5 to −20 degrees. But shelter along the Michigan shoreline is scarce. Winds howl, exposing bare ground for sustained periods of time. And so we gardening folk worry.

Such angst comes with the territory. Gardening presumes a certain level of risk. Climate zones are not an exact science. Plants as well as gardeners are capable of misreading the signs.

Getting by with a Little Help

But snow is not the enemy in cold climates. It can protect a plant against brutal wind chills. Break out the snow fences to trap accumulations and stabilize an area that is vulnerable to freeze-thaw problems. Fresh mulch also works, but it pays to avoid use of garden 'waste' that can lead to rot and plant diseases. Molds can cause more damage than exposing perennials to the elements.

If a gardener becomes too obsessed with plant safety, it takes a lot of fun out of the process of plant choice. In so-called micro-climates, protected from the wind and warmed by steady sunlight, it is amazing what plants can survive even outside their 'comfort zones'.

We all have our stories. So do our gardens. Sharing such a wealth of experience forges precious bonds that can put to rest our angst about our failure as gardeners. Our collective love affair with the earth can transcend time, weather and the forces of nature with which and against which a gardener constantly works and struggles.

Gardening over the years from Michigan to New York, Pennsylvania, Iowa and Arizona, I know how those very first Ice Age farmers felt as the glaciers began to shrink around them. They too must have worried for those tender plants they were so tentatively learning to cultivate. Climates change. The gardener's heart? Not so much.

March

In a spectacular display, a tulip opens to the sun in the author's garden, Long Island, New York.

O FORTUNA
First published March, 2013

March is roaring in like a lion. After last year's drought conditions in the Upper Midwest, farmers certainly appreciate the largesse of white stuff. But for die-hard gardeners, spring may seem farther away than ever.

One of my favorite 'spring' stories comes from my husband's days as a grad student at the University of Chicago. His roommate, who already had a Master's degree in chemistry, wound up at Chicago on a full scholarship to encourage students from non-traditional fields to pursue a theology degree. With uncommon gusto, the guy threw himself into reading the Great Books and wisdom of the ages.

Now as then, Chicago was notorious for its howling wind chills and monumental lake-effect snows. By March, cabin fever was rampant on campus. When finally the weather reporters announced a genuine thaw—or at least when temperatures stayed above freezing for a week running—the roommate announced that it was time to celebrate.

The guy threw open the window of their dorm room and started to play a recording of Carl Off's tribute to medieval life and love, *Carmina Burana*. Full-blast. He bought a liter of Portuguese wine, then stripped to his birthday suit and climbed out on the sunny window ledge to consume it. Snow thawed. Earth awakened. Spring was coming.

Gardeners love the spring solstice. Years ago we moved to Long Island for the first time and I couldn't believe my good fortune. Thanks to the Gulf Stream, late March and early April were delightfully warm. So by mid-April, I had transferred the seedlings in my indoor flats to the garden. Then I promptly sat back and watched them rot in the ground as rain and ground fog took their toll. No point in rushing the season.

Gardening is not an occupation for the faint of heart. Instant gratification is rare. What we want and what we need as gardeners are not always the same. We yearn for spring, all the while knowing that without vigorous snowfalls, our perennials will suffer. Too warm and early a thaw can decimate whole crops. There is a rhythm to life that needs to prevail, regardless of how depressing our personal case of cabin fever might be.

O fortune, like the moon, you are ever changeable, the 13th century Latin poet wrote in *Carmina Burana*. He certainly knew his stuff. Over 800 years later, that same song topped the chart of most-played classical pieces in Great Britain—a run of more than 75 years! Not surprising, the Brits consider themselves a Nation of Gardeners.

Jack-in-the-Pulpit commands a shady spot in the Bay View Memorial Garden, Michigan.

TEAM SPORTS
First published in March, 2007

Seed catalogs boast a wealth of riches. But most intriguing to me are not the individual plants, but the illustrations or plans for how a variety of seeds or plants can create a whole garden for any and all conditions, sun or shade. One plant does not a garden make.

Community and diversity are the natural state of things in a garden. Plants do not exist in isolation. And as they jostle for space or nutrients, their interdependence is life-changing for the whole garden. Growth and change and the need to share become daily facts of life.

We can learn a lot from how gardens grow. Successful garden design relies on healthy teamwork. Border plants may not be the flashiest plants, but they are crucial to hold the line between lawn and bed. Sturdy, compact species can work better than external stakes to support taller, more fragile stalks. Each plant has its own contribution to make.

There is no rule either that people need to garden alone. Community gardening becomes a great way to promote that kind of sharing. Each member of the garden team has a unique role to play, promoting a healthy sense of personal self-worth and mutual respect. Our backs may not sustain prolonged digging, but we can contribute the patience of a weeder or dead-header, cutting back the bloomed-out and weather-damaged. Mutual team support becomes part of the experience.

A wise crew leader knows this and tries to pair workers in small groups rather than just deploying people individually in isolated parts of the garden. The relationships that result can be far more powerful as motivators than just checking off tasks on a to-do list.

Gardening alone, there is temptation to become obsessed with 'how big' and 'how much' a plot of ground can produce. In a community garden, the goal is not the spectacular achievement of a single plant or bed or even gardener, but on the *whole*.

At root and branch, the gardening life is not a *competition*, but a *contact* sport. Competitiveness becomes a lonely, divisive business. It magnifies our faults as well as our accomplishments. Gardening can teach us a very different way of relating, where community, cooperation and connectedness prevail—not just among plants, but those who tend them.

Where there is a bare plot of earth, a garden waits to bloom. And gardening begins with community. March might not be the season to get out and plant. But it is never too early or late to cultivate a friend.

First published in March, 2012

Travel is good for the gardener soul in all of us. Within hours or days, travelers can experience a too-early spring in Louisiana and Mississippi that leaves tourism officials worrying how to stage azalea festivals when these spectacular bushes had already bloomed themselves out weeks earlier. Meanwhile, Lake Effect snow is raging on the Michigan shores.

Travel blurs the seasons, wrenches us out of the everyday, forces us to rethink the 'norm'. My husband has taken to calling these times on the road "Wow!" garden moments. I like that concept.

We perennial gardeners, especially, tend to be creatures of habit. Plants become old friends. While perennials may have their quirks, gardeners depend on their steadying presence. On a deep spiritual level, gardens offer a sense of stability in a most unstable world.

The rhythm of the growing season can provide another anchor. But woe to us if we take it for granted. Late winter blasts and early frosts quickly jolt us out of that complacency. I like to think such wake-up calls represent the garden's unique potential for surprise, mystery and even the childlike joy of discovery. The Wow-factor is out there, if we are prepared to recognize it when and where we see it.

A friend in California gave me several cactus shoots which right now are languishing in a beat-up six-inch plastic potting container in our motor home sink. Very little light comes in through the window of the galley kitchen. I had my doubts about the poor thing's chances. Then out of the blue several days ago came that Wow! moment. At the dark base of one of the shoots, a fat bud-like appendage appeared. It keeps growing. And then yesterday near that parent shoot, first two and then a third straight-as-an-arrow new shoots appeared. And then a spine.

Never presume. On a road trip along the Natchez Trace, bold yellow flowers peppering a meadow reminded me of the wild mustard dotting the Michigan landscape. But even from a distance, I could tell these flowers were larger, more massive. *Butterweed*, a park ranger tells me as I capture the fleabane-like flower heads with the close-up lens of my camera. I also learn an odd looking white wildflower is a form of garlic, very different from the tall-stalked variety growing in my garden.

Gardens are never simple. They shock. They confuse. They mystify. Gardens make us sit up and take notice. Maybe it's why we love them. Like life, perhaps? Gardeners understand that better than anyone.

After a slow start, one of the author's favorites, hellebore [Christmas or Lenten roses] flourished in the author's New York garden. Transplanting things is not always easy.

THE LANGUAGE OF FLOWERS

First published in March, 2007

As a community garden volunteer, I don't give too much thought to what perennials are my favorites. My job on the crew is to nurture the plants chosen by our garden planner. Since we are creating a memorial garden, definite rules apply about what to include.

A major design principle in a memorial garden is use of color. Yellows and reds are considered too passionate and showy. Instead, the palette includes cool purples and blues, mauve and pinks which tend toward the blue, as well as pristine whites.

Such links between plants and the emotions are nothing new. One of the most famous lists of flowers and their significance occurs in Shakespeare's *Hamlet*. The doomed heroine Ophelia gifts the courtiers with freshly picked blossoms while sharing the poignant emotional significance of each of them. Later, in Victorian times, people were obsessed with the language or lexicon of different plants and flowers.

To this day, roses are seen as classic symbols of love. Pink varieties convey admiration and appreciation. Red expresses romance, passion or can honor achievement. White stands for innocence and humble grace. Yellow roses can express 'welcome home' or friendship, but beware—they also can symbolize jealousy.

Even ordinary garden plants have assigned meanings, such as daisies (innocence and loyalty) and the iris (faith, courage). A whole emotional vocabulary has sprung up around carnations, the official flower of Mother's Day. Pink says, "I will never forget you", while red says, "my heart aches for you". White symbolizes pure affection. Yellow or striped carnations can symbolize disappointment or rejection.

Not all plants have assigned meanings. If I could choose them for some of my garden favorites, they would be: Daffodils—*unpretentious*; Prairie Asters—*persistence*; Astilbes—*gracefulness*; Coneflower—*joyous simplicity*; Day lilies—*exuberance*; Foxglove—*mystery*; Lupine—*frustration* (at least I sure have a dickens of a time growing them!).

In every season, we have a perfect chance to tell the gardener in our lives how we feel. Cut flowers can be wonderful for doing that year-round. But so can the living gift of in-the-pot perennials. With luck, I can keep them going strong indoors until it's time for them to go outside in the garden. May they flower for years to come.

Foxglove and Columbine interact to create a whimsical, mutually supportive plant community in the author's New York garden.

The joy of gardening is not just about exercise, fresh air and healthy levels of Vitamin D from all that sun, or even the beauty that results. Many gardeners cultivate personal rituals or traditions that can transform the science of gardening into not just an art form but a spiritual exercise.

Rite of Spring

With the first March thaw, one of my favorite rituals begins. At first light or when the sun reaches its height for the day, it's time to stroll the garden looking for signs of life. Whether weeds or perennials, that isn't important. What matters is to catch a glimpse of the first tiny shoots braving the last of the winter chill. A first sighting of the sturdy lobes of the daffodils or the thinner blades of the crocus shoots is a better antidote to the winter blahs than a tonic. Spring is coming.

I Come to the Garden Alone

It's no accident that one of the most popular American folk hymns talks about the joy of strolling the morning or evening garden to catch a glimpse of the Divine. The feel and scent of mossy, cool garden air can have an incredible calming effect on the troubled or weary spirit. A prayer by any other name, garden walks are a grounding experience. They make every sweaty weeding session to come a lot less painful.

Love in any Language

For centuries, herb as well as perennial gardeners have fixed upon a common lexicon for what particular plants signify, not just for a garden but the gardener. Learning to appreciate traditions like the Victorian *Book of Flowers* adds a whole new dimension to the gardening experience. In any language, plants are about relationships.

Connecting the Dots

In the garden, time and space converge. Gardeners know immediately what poets mean by the rhythm of the seasons or the 'season round'. The traditional shape of herb gardens is the circle. Connecting the four cardinal points as triangles will create a star within the circular design. Traditions like the Yule log are as old as the Druids. German 'May wine' dates back to the flowering of woodruff in ancient Teutonic forests. In gardening lore, there is a story and season for everything.

Every time I open the garage door, a stash of tools reminds me another gardening season is coming. Bottom line for my spiritual life: hope. Life doesn't get any more livable or meaningful than that.

Living sunshine. The cheerful faces of narcissus, a herald of spring, turn toward the sky in the author's New York garden.

April

Bud break is an eagerly awaited event in the vineyards on Long Island, New York.

THE POWER OF GREEN
First published in April, 2011

Hope is green, an old German proverb says. I believe it. As a gardener, the first sight of the daffodil and crocus spears thrusting up through the icy ground makes me positively giddy. Images of spring and the garden color our language, the poetry of our everyday.

Searches for quotable quotes about gardens and spring yield an abundance of riches. There's that old chestnut, *budding prospects.* The ultimate insult *no spring chicken* popped into our language as early as the 1700s. Even earlier, in Old English, the word *green* itself is related to the verb *groan,* 'to grow'.

I mentioned my obsession with the signs and language of spring out loud the other day. I discovered I wasn't alone. "Willows," my friend blurted out. "Willow-green. I spotted it yesterday. The willows are really greening up. You know, that funny neon-yellowy-green. There's nothing quite like it!"

She was dead-right. As for me, the sight of crocus blooming wildly in the snow hits me like a sunny day after weeks of rain. Sheltered by the foundation of the garage, a carpet of snowdrops conjure up visions of a medieval walled garden. And at the onset of April rains, my inner G.P.S. begins to track signs of willow greens in lawns and open fields.

Apparently the choice of green ink as a color for U.S. money in the 19th century was strictly pragmatic, an attempt to foil counterfeiters. You could have fooled me. In today's shaky economic times, there is something fiscally reassuring about talk of 'green things growing'. And after decades of wholesale flight from the land in the U.S., a whole new generation of young entrepreneurs is rediscovering agriculture as a profession. Inflation hasn't spared the gardening business (seed packets cost nearly two bucks now). Still, they're worth every penny and a great deal cheaper and healthier in the long run than tranquilizers.

Grounding we call that instinctive fascination with things that center or draw us toward the Great Eternal. "If winter comes," the English poet Percy Bysshe Shelley wrote, "can spring be far behind?" The reverse also applies. Our journey through the seasons leads invariably to fall and earth's long winter's sleep—preludes to yet another awakening.

However we describe it, the siren call of the spring garden couldn't be more timely. It has been a long, hard winter. High time, I tell myself, to get off the computer and out in the garden.

Millions and millions of stars. **Allium, a member of the onion family, adds an exotic touch to the Bay View Memorial Garden, Michigan.**

GROWING THINGS
Collected thoughts from April, 2014 - May, 2011 - May, 2012

Gardening folk, especially in the bleak mid-winter, depend on their hardy faith to get them through. In the face of howling winds, the imagination conjures up visions of things unseen. The solstice is upon us. Change spells growth. And when people like plants cease to grow, they die.

Time in a garden is not all sunshine and roses. Late April snowfalls and winter assert themselves just when spring should come. The garden suddenly struggles under bitter winds and another round of brutal chills. Promise of an early spring seems cruel, even sadistic.

The plight of the April gardens is life writ large. New possibilities do not emerge without their share of travail. Forces, both for good and ill, are at work beyond a garden's control. I believe it is no accident that major religious festivals in the Jewish and Christian tradition are playing themselves out even as I write. The garden quietly teaches us to endure. Life without hope is barren ground, indeed.

And so, inside dim-lit sanctuaries in this season, lilies bloom, crocuses and daffodils—symbols of humanity's deepest hopes. Shoots, leaves, buds and blossoms inspire the longing heart to triumph over life's darkest winter. Whatever comes, we can flower where we are planted.

In the Bulb Lies a Flower

When it comes to spring, the watch word is Patience. My generation claimed to want the world and want it now. Life rarely works that way. Carried to extremes, such hedonism can lead to what critics call the 'rampant narcissism' at work in contemporary life. Witness those once-idealistic folks in my age bracket who now brag that they are spending their kids' inheritance, without thought for tomorrow.

In the garden, the poor narcissus is anything but a symbol of easy, self-absorbed living. Although it is among the earliest to bloom, it really has to work at it. Often the plant's graceful leaves bear the scars of the effort, the legacy of searing frosts and howling winds.

Instant gratification has its appeal. I would love a 'pill' that would melt the pounds and inches without all the sweat and angst. But the things I treasure the most in life didn't come about that way: building strong relationships, childbirth or a lifetime's work of which I can be proud. The best things in life do not lend themselves to quick fixes.

So, here's to spring, whenever it chooses to come. Gardeners cope. Their passion is not just about the soil underfoot but about the soul.

Feathery foliage and the distinctive blunt-cut petals of Dwarf Creeping Phlox serve as a lush border planting in the author's New York garden.

A hardy 'Winter' Gardenia thrives in a sheltered spot in a friend's garden, Long Island, New York. Waxy leaves and large flowers are as eye-catching as the vivid red petals.

One of my all-time favorite Monty Python skits is the infamous "Parrot Sketch". The bird ain't dead, just resting. We laugh in part because it captures the lengths to which we will go—delusional at times—to avoid the obvious. Things age, die. Ultimately, we all face that same reality.

Part of the appeal of gardening is that it quietly debunks our tendencies to deny the basic rhythms of life. Beautiful as this summer's annuals were, they will not be back. If the winter gets too nasty, we even begin to worry about the perennials. When soil is depleted, it too needs renewal. Sobering stuff. Still, as gardeners we learn to pick ourselves up, replant and cultivate. And we continue to hope.

Our world is experiencing a powerful wake-up call, discovering a lot about limits, especially in the global economy and environment. Such hard truths make us question our capacity to live honestly, within realistic boundaries, and reassess what really matters in life.

Like many semi-retirees, I find myself watching the stock index with a skeptical eye, well aware how much life can and likely will change in the months and years ahead. And when it all becomes too discouraging, I pick up a garden catalog and begin to dream.

We are no longer a pastoral society where survival is measured by the actions, wise or foolish, of a handful of people in frontier villages or the capacity of a plot of ground in the back yard to feed a planet. Life has changed. But some things are constant, all the same.

A seed goes into the ground, and if tended faithfully, grows. A flower buds, blossoms gloriously and fades. Even in its passing, it enriches the soil around it. No excesses here, unless it is the unexpected largesse of zucchinis left on an unsuspecting neighbor's porch.

In these ambivalent times, one of the greatest gifts we can give to coming generations is the legacy of gardening. Gardening is the ultimate reality check. It is hard to fake a balance sheet in a flower bed. More often than not, we reap what we sow. The values I learned gardening alongside my own grandmother have never seemed more relevant. *Patience. Commitment. Good stewardship. Respect for the earth. Gratitude for the beauty of a rose drenched in morning dew.*

Inspired by the First Lady and White House chef, a vegetable garden has been planted on the White House lawn. I vote we insist that our elected officials each take turns nurturing and caring for it.

41

Clematis unfolds as a stunning surprise among the ivy climbing the pergola in the author's garden, Long Island, New York.

FOR EVERYTHING A SEASON

First published in April, 2012

I don't know what is more frustrating as a gardener: knowing it is too cold to plant or prematurely assuming that winter is over for good. Watching bulbs sprout and flower a month too soon may get my gardener's heart beating faster. But after several such years of unusually warm and early springs, it seemed all the worse when several brutal winters in a row hit the region.

I learned the hard way to appreciate what 'seasons' meant when we moved to New York decades ago. Long Island, I told myself, is not Buffalo, even in the worst of winters. With the Gulf Stream flowing off its southern shore, the Island's climate is actually quite mild—more so than New York City and certainly the rest of the New England coast. We spent our first snowless Christmas outdoors, minus jackets and in shirt sleeves. Quite a contrast to our years sojourning in the Upper Midwest!

Ground on Long Island never freezes to any depth. So when the threat of snow and hard frosts seemed over by March, the gardener in me did cartwheels. I chafed at the bit to start gardening. Finally in early April, I broke ground and started planting. And then the rains came, one damp and gray day after the next. Shoes in the closet began to mold. Come mid-May, all those seeds in my garden had rotted in the ground. Sadder but wiser, I had to start over and plant again.

Ag Extension folk in Michigan recently warned that the upper part of the state is now one temperature zone warmer. Global warming may be changing the face of our climate, but just when we think we have things figured out, temperatures plummet to record lows in January.

For everything there is a season. *Season* crept into Middle English and Old French around 1200 to 1300 AD, apparently from the Latin for 'sowing'. The word also quickly came to mean 'make palatable by aging.' We season our food. Our lives season or ripen with time.

As we cultivate our gardens, it pays to respect the concept of *timing*. Successful gardeners walk that very fine line between hope and the common sense that comes with experience. Love is that way, says author Ann Bronte in her amazingly modern 1848 novel, *Tenant of Wildfell Hall*. Hope lives, despite and because of the sometimes painful life lessons that accumulate along the way.

There is a time for planting. There is a time to wait. And ah, for the wisdom, to know the difference.

An energetic bee uses Cosmos as a landing pad in the author's New York garden.

May

Desert flowers thrive among the thorns in a garden
near the author's Tempe, Arizona home.

Clematis petals glow like shards of stained glass in the late afternoon sun on a fence in a Michigan garden.

Fences make good neighbors, Robert Frost once wrote. Much as I love his poetry, here he and I part ways. Gardens, not chain link or pickets, build healthy community, one stalk and blossom at a time.

Gardens soften the hard edges of lot lines. They add color and whimsy to the monochrome expanses of green that divide us. It is hard to fight over whose dandelions are aggressing across the backyards when neighbors are standing together admiring each other's hollyhocks or coneflowers.

Newcomers invading the neighborhood? Hearty welcomes are not limited to pies on the doorstep. Just pot a couple of iris in a sawed-off milk carton and trim it out with tin foil and a festive bow. Then plop the gift down on the front stoop and watch the smiles. A garden is born.

One winter in New York, a reckless driver plowed off the road, through the neighbor's yard and into our basement (a terrifying way for us to wake up at 1:39 AM). My heart felt a whole lot better next day when a neighbor brought over a little pot full of miniature daffodils in bloom. "I just thought you might need these," she said.

It took some time for the ground to soften enough for the contractor to repair the hole in our house. But when he did, I transplanted those bulbs in the flower bed. The tire track scars disappeared in no time!

Perennial gardens, especially, are a gift that just keep on giving. What better defines 'neighborliness' than to thin out sprawling clumps of plants, then share the excess with a friend. Or simply set the goodies out at the curb with a sign that says, FREE. . .AND HAPPY GARDENING! Guaranteed, the plants will walk. I find great comfort in picturing some grim or empty corner of the world made a little brighter with those pesky little Obedient Plants that just could not seem to behave for me.

Some years back on Long Island, one of the oldest communities in the country lobbied for zoning laws to stop the spread of Hampton-style fencing—by banning 15-foot arbor vitae hedges. Plants are not meant to divide but bring us together. My hats off to those folk for the foresight to try to preserve good-old-fashioned neighborliness.

Fortunately, when our own neighbors' wood lattice screen fell down, they decided not to rebuild. Instead, together we spent warm spring days plotting ways to create a garden—theirs and ours—to grace that vacant space between us.

HARD TIMES SURVIVAL GUIDE
First published in May, 2009

The physical and emotional 'feel' of visiting a shaded bed of hostas is very different from confronting a mound of daisies swaying in the summer sun. Gardens appeal not just to the eyes, but to all the senses.

Scientists say that from cradle to grave, the most basic sense is smell. Smell also is tied closely to our sense of taste. In the dew-drenched splendor of the morning garden, there is nothing quite like breathing in the heady scent of lavender. At once herb and flower, lavender's gray tinged leaves and spiky purple blossoms provide a subtle feast for the taste buds, as well as smell and sight. Chefs often use fragrant flowers like rose petals as garnish or in salads. (Note: always consult edible flower lists to make sure a particular species is safe for human consumption.)

Walking a garden is also a tactile adventure. When we bend to gaze into a lily's trumpet, the velvety pollen clings tenaciously to our skin as if applied with an artist's brush. That touch is pure gold.

At times the garden is so still, the listener can almost hear the plants growing. Subtle as the rising wind, grasses rustle around us. The rhythm of life plays itself out in a symphony of growth and flowering. We hear time's passing, fleeting and yet somehow eternal.

The formal structure of a classic French garden conveys reason and calm. The calculated 'wildness' of the English garden transports a visitor to a simpler, rustic time and place. A sprawling prairie or wildflower garden evokes a sense of nature removed from the intervention of man. None of those designs happen by accident. Informality takes as much planning as the planes, angles and geometric beds of the formal garden.

Tending a Memorial Garden is an especially profound sensual and spiritual experience. The palette of the flowering plants is unique—all violets and blues, wines and pinks and pristine whites. No brash reds, yellows or oranges intrude on the scene. The colors evoke not passion, but quiet contemplation and rest.

Touch, smell, taste, hearing, sight. The lush morning garden speaks of creation and dawning—our primal ancestors walking with the Divine in their long ago Eden. Life is all around us, our senses remind us. We are a privileged part of it. And at the close of the day, the sleeping garden rustles with blossoms folding in upon themselves against the chill. Even the sunset of life has a quiet beauty all its own.

Iris leaves look as showy as the flowers in the author's garden on Long Island, New York.

Bellflower [Campanula Carpatica] serves as a border plant in this Appleton, Wisconsin garden, the author's hometown.

GARDENS DON'T RETIRE

First published in May, 2013

A lot of planning goes into retirement, from financial issues to health care and sustainable living arrangements. For the avid gardener, retirement presents special challenges that can have enormous impact on both one's physical and even spiritual well-being.

Condo or apartment living can have a powerful appeal after decades of struggling with exterior maintenance, snow removal and lawn care. But when it comes to giving up the family garden, change can be tough. Gardens are not just about 'landscaping'. For most gardeners, tending their beds fills a deep physical, emotional and spiritual need.

True, age catches up with us all. What was easy to maintain for a gardener at 40 or 50 can be a back-breaker at 60 and older. But that awareness does not necessarily soften the transition from a single family home and garden to communal lawns and plantings. Perennials become 'friends' and the beds around them precious landmarks that literally ground a gardener's life. As a result, some condo and townhouse communities wisely promote volunteer participation on grounds committees, organize communal gardens or permit pot gardening.

Snowbirds often experience that kind of soul-crisis when they look for outlets for their gardening instincts. Familiar or favorite plant varieties may or may not survive in radically different climates. And northern gardeners who have no trouble investing in flats of summer annuals may balk at the seasonal throw-away patterns of Southwest gardeners. Arizona garden stores haul out their 'spring' stock in early February, but by June, those plants already struggle with the heat. After the die-off, another wave of 'annuals' shows up in September. Adjusting to such radically different calendars, as well as to the vagaries of drip irrigation, can be problematic.

After her move from Wisconsin to Arizona, my mom—a lifelong gardener—vowed to 'give up gardening' for good. Our housewarming gift to her was a pot full of petunias. At first it was tricky for her to get in the rhythm of watering both mornings and evenings. But the reaction of her neighbors to that glorious pot garden of hers quickly became a source of pride.

There is no retirement from gardening, any more than retirement from life. Gardening gets in our blood, sustains and keeps us in touch with our best selves—wherever 'home' becomes. Gardening defines us.

Zinnias, an annual, have become a much-admired fixture along the fence of a historic Victorian Inn in Bay View, Michigan, reappearing season after season.

IT'S ALL A MATTER OF SCALE
First published in May, 2008

Something new is blooming in my garden. For years my long-suffering spouse has been helping me dig, weed, transplant—that, despite the fact he is allergic to most flowers and has a back even worse than mine. Given his druthers, he would plant all hostas or ground cover. Still, he pitches in for spring and fall cleanup. If that isn't loyalty, I don't know what is.

For years, his personal 'gardening' has been to tend two ponds. One is the size of a large picnic table, the other a washtub. Still, he had some interesting flora growing out there and one very tough goldfish (a former 10-cent feeder fish rescued from the pet store). It took my husband seven years, but a family of frogs finally moved in as well.

All that is changing, big time. Several summers ago when I built an HO-gauge railroad in our cottage dining room with my grandson, I couldn't help spot the wistful looks from my hubby. I got the hint. For Christmas, Valentine's and every holiday in between, I gifted him with a G-scale garden railroad. And before I could say, *where's the shovel*, he had carved out a 15- by 10-foot network of tracks for engines, rail cars and a trolley happily chugging back and forth on a track of its own.

It's an amazing engineering feat, not quite the Brooklyn Bridge but close. Kit-bashed bird houses create buildings to scale. Magically, plants also chosen to scale make the layout come alive, greenery that resembles full-size bushes and trees.

Gardening an Inch to the Foot

It's my turn to provide technical support. When I now prowl garden stores, it is literally with a whole new perspective. Trick is to find slow and low growth plants, ones with both small leaves and flowers when they mature. When it comes to rocky hillsides and lawns for garden-rail structures, some mosses and lichen are perfect.

Suddenly I also have acquired a great appreciation for dwarf species like phlox and Creeping Jenny. Herbs like dwarf oregano can survive even in cold climates and make perfect 'miniature' ground covers. We have yet to integrate a working water feature into the layout, but that is next.

I am not advocating we all dig up our perennials and start laying track. But our garden rail experience taught me a valuable lesson. One guy's chore is another guy's recreation. And so-called 'traditional' garden plants are a lot more diverse and versatile than we think.

A frog family sets up housekeeping in the pond of the author's Long Island, New York back yard.

June

Cosmos floats on a sea of its feathery foliage in the author's garden on Long Island, New York.

BECOMING WHAT WE PLANT
First published in June, 2014

As we walk the beds, surveying the carnage after a long, hard winter, we contemplate choices that will shape our gardens for not just the summer, but the future. And *how* we garden will also say a lot about us.

There are bound to be holes, perhaps even lots of them among the perennials. Do we invest in annuals to fill those holes? Some might see that as a 'quick fix' mindset. Others see it as an instinct to live in the now, to celebrate seasonal beauty even in the face of devastating loss. An infusion of annuals also can give the garden precious time to heal itself.

Then there is the question of whether to replant exactly what succumbed to the pressures of a hard winter. Some gardeners quickly say, Enough. It is time to try something else. Others persist, give the fragile varieties that died out a second chance, maybe grasping at a slightly more hardy version of the perennials that were lost. Either way, like life, gardening is a risk. Whatever the choice, gardening is an investment of hope in the future.

While some plants suffer, others rush to fill the gap. Such perennials can be called *invasive*. But then maybe they are just opportunists or survivors. It all depends on how we look at their role. Gardeners may need to intervene lest the garden become boringly one-dimensional. Gardens thrive on diversity. The ultimate challenge is to make sure conditions are right for that rich culture to flourish.

To weed or not to weed, that is the question. The long-time crew chief of a Michigan community garden loves to say of weeding, "If you get 'em first time out, the job is easier all season." True enough, but the gardener still needs to decide how much ambivalence to tolerate. Some gardeners leave bare dirt between everything to define where one stand of perennials ends and another begins—much like the highly cultivated French garden style. Personally, I have always favored the British school that tends to let the plants duke it out, growing together, leaning on one another for support, creating a flowering community that seems to have sprung up that way naturally, without human intervention.

Bottom line, there is beauty in all of it. As an art form, gardening is not just about healthy plants or a steady succession of flowering through the seasons. The garden we cultivate becomes a model of how we visualize the ideal community. And that is profound spiritual stuff—something thoughtful gardeners learn to appreciate and treasure.

Droplets glisten on the petals of a peony nestled in a
bed of Wild Geranium in a Northern Michigan garden.

WHEN ENOUGH IS ENOUGH
A column lost to the Great Computer in the Sky

Like people, some plants are aggressive. Others get lost in the crowd. Some wilt under the harsh glare of noonday, or like hostas, they rack up a nasty case of sunburn. Others fight back when rooted in the shade, their stems or branches thrusting up in claw-fingered appeal toward the light.

Life in the garden is about struggle, growth and the quest to build a beautiful, healthy community. The master gardener's job—an executive, legislative and judicial role all in one—becomes to keep the aggressors in bounds. Brash and cocky entrepreneurs of the perennial world will rush to fill any space allotted to them. No shrinking violets here. Self-starters mean low maintenance. That's a good thing, right?

Call it tenderhearted or short-sighted, but I find it hard to whack away at otherwise healthy perennials just because they get a little uppity about sharing. I procrastinate. And for all the warning labels on the pot label at the nursery about 'invasive', I find myself subconsciously rationalizing, "Well, that one's a survivor!"

It became time to second-guess that laissez faire style when the only plants left around our pond were water celery and some ornamental mystery-grass. Bleeding heart and lungwort were inexplicably missing-in-action. Roots of the Siberian iris and some daisy-like invader became so entangled, that to separate them would take an axe. Apparently a Korean import Houttuynia cordata, with its Joseph's-coat coloring and tiny white flowers, is hell bent on world domination. And then there's lamium.

It isn't easy to sense at what point encroachment becomes something more sinister. The invasive species just keep testing and probing until one day, the gardener has to say, *Enough*. Foresight helps as well. Some plant choices make for better neighbors than others.

I hit the crisis point in my garden this week, starting with a resolve to beat back the prairie asters creeping into the more fragile coreopsis. I can't prove it, but I swear that the digitalis [*aka* Fox Glove] somehow 'did in' my strawberries. Cutting my loses, I transplanted the few survivors to safer ground in a raised, boxed bed.

Play nice, our Moms taught us. There hasn't been a lot of that going around in the world lately. And collectively, we human beings have spent a lot of time in denial, reluctant to mess with the balance of things. It isn't smart, a gardener discovers, to do that forever. As in the rest of life, there comes a time to break out the spades and shovels.

Golden beds of Oenothera [Evening Primrose] splash
rays of living sunshine through the author's garden,
Long Island, New York.

STAY-CATIONS ... GARDENER STYLE

First published in June, 2008

When gas prices soar or our budgets rebel at the notion of an away-vacation, folks like me with the travel bug find ourselves quickly searching for creative ways of satisfying our wanderlust without breaking the bank. One possibility—to revisit my garden, not as 'gardener' but as an incidental tourist to renew and recharge my batteries.

At first light, the grass feels deliciously cool underfoot. Teardrops glisten on the leaves and blossoms as they turn their faces to the rising sun. Night shadows fade. All is hushed and still, expectant, welcoming the new day. The perfume of unfolding buds drifts on the breeze.

From among the astilbe with its delicate, Arabian Nights foliage, a lone obedient plant has popped up its head where it hadn't been the day before. Anything but obedient, I chuckle to myself. High comedy reigns where I would have least expected it, right here in my own backyard.

High noon I retrace my steps. Shimmering waves of mid-day heat transform the bed of daisies into a glassy tropical sea. The air is moist and heavy with green, a breath of the rain forest.

I am not alone on my junket. Ponderous in flight, bees move to a droning cadence from flower to flower. Velvety butterflies swoop and soar, all restless energy. In the pine branches overhead, the shadow of a hawk contemplates its lunch scurrying for cover under an elephant-leaved hosta. A gentle breeze shakes the coral bells.

The day is fading, in a sunset blaze of oranges and purples. Weary petals curl in upon themselves. Twilight descends like a blanket pulled tight against the gathering dark. The ponderous silhouettes of the delphinium rise up against the horizon like the foothills of some mountain range stretching out to infinity.

Quicksilver light dances over the sleeping garden. The moon is full. I, too, feel a weariness that makes me think of bed. In a single day, my journeys have taken me from the far reaches of the Orient to the equator to the blue Appalachian ranges No travel agency could have plotted an itinerary as creative or inspiring as those moments walking the garden. Learning to see with new eyes becomes the ultimate adventure.

When the Creator walked the garden, the ancient text reassures us, life was found to be good—every precious blade, every leaf, every stalk and stem and flower. And as Eden's long day came to an end, the Creator too found in the garden a place of peace and rest.

First published in June, 2012

I was a late bloomer. During my teenage years, one of the most irritating questions that adults shot in my direction was, "What do you want to be when you grow up?" I had no clue.

At seventy-something, I still don't. But all those decades later, at least I have found an answer to that nagging challenge. Growing up, I would answer, is a lifelong process. It takes time and patience. And not even the wisest of us can imagine how and when we will bloom where we are planted over the years.

Plants are very good teachers. When most perennials first pop up, it is difficult and sometimes virtually impossible to tell one from the other. Hasty judgments when weeding the spring garden can be fatal. Most gardeners have their share of war stories about rooting out the new baby plants that they thought were weeds.

It is only when plants get their *second* or "true leaves", that a gardener can begin to tell what the perennial is going to look like as an adult plant. I look back at my own career and personal life and realize how little I suspected what I would become. But in the end, I would not have traded that journey, with all its twists and turns, for anything.

In drought years or planted in too deep a shade, plants try their darndest to compensate. They grow spindly and tall, straining for the sun. Leaves may yellow and wilt, but for all that, plants are remarkably resilient. Just when we think a plant is past its prime, barely worthy of fertilizer, it roars back to life with a vengeance, engineering a record growth-spurt with a new-found sense of purpose.

Which is why gardening with young children is one of the most precious gifts a parent, grandparent or other adult can bestow. Growing our own food teaches self-reliance. Tending a flowering perennial teaches the joys of adding beauty to even the barest patch of dirt.

Gardens promote the art of loving, cultivating and nurturing. Everything on this earth needs a bit of help to grow. The myth of the totally self-made human being is just that—a myth. Love and care will pay back that investment a thousand-fold.

Gardening teaches us all that and more. When I watch those struggling shoots and seedlings trying to grow their second leaves, I feel a powerful empathy, even kinship. Whatever comes, they try their best to bloom where they are planted. That challenge is downright human.

Spiderwort triggers memories of growing up in Wisconsin, gardening alongside my mother and grandmother. Three-petal flowering plants are rare. But tied to my images of childhood, the stunning purple flowers and spiky leaves are as down-home as lightning bugs ('thunder bugs' as our granddaughter calls them) dancing in the summer night.

REMEMBRANCE

First published in June, 2010

Memorial Day. As a girl growing up in Wisconsin, this was the time to load up the trunk of the car with geraniums and head out into the rural countryside to decorate the grave sites of family—many of whom I had never met. Nowadays after the holiday passes, these quiet resting places bloom with plastic and silk, a concession to scattered families and lives.

This week I came across fragments of an amazing obituary from somewhere in Canada. Instead of sending flowers as a memorial, it read, spend time in a garden. What an incredible tribute for anyone we love or have loved, a way to celebrate a life well and truly lived. And what a powerful message of love and hope it offers in this season of remembrance.

Take time to enjoy, that obituary urges. Life can be a struggle. Yet, beauty is still there to experience—provided we recognize and embrace it for what it is. The richness and happiness we find in a garden doesn't require a fat bank account or brass engraved nameplates. In a culture driven by over-achievement, there are times our greatest success may be our capacity to sit up and take notice.

Search for permanence in the ephemeral. Setting a plant or seed or seedling into the ground is the consummate act of faith. Gardeners are not naive enough to assume life is easy. Stuff happens. YouTube brings us images of baseball-sized hail that plummets into a suburban swimming pool in Oklahoma like boulders tossed into a pond. Straight-line winds topple hundred-year-old evergreens. And still gardeners plant—faithfully cultivate growth if only for a season.

Redefine what it means to lean on each other. Even when the rains come hard and fast, my iris haven't given up. Heavy with bloom, the bent stalks draw their support from the sprawling, leafy mounds of day lilies behind them. Gardens teach us about community writ large and the inclusive and reciprocal power of sharing. To give is important. It is no less a grace to learn how to receive.

Cultivate the NOW. Life doesn't come equipped with Pause buttons. Who knows when petals will begin to fall? We need to stop and marvel when and where we can.

If we yearn to honor what is important in our lives, we would do well to spend time in a garden. I can't think of a better, more fitting memorial to life, the things or people we value and love.

Mediterranean Bells Allium [Allium nectaroscordum siculum] stands like a living carillon in the Bay View Memorial Garden, Michigan. Behold the lowly onion.

A water Lily floats like a starburst of petals in the author's pond garden, Long Island, New York.

Summer Fireworks. Allium Schubertii ushers in the
Fourth in the Bay View Memorial Garden, Michigan.

Happy birthday, USA. The most mail I ever received in response to a column was one in which I suggested that it should be mandatory for all political candidates to spend time working in a garden. With the country struggling more or less in permanent electioneering mode, I can't think of a better way to build the kind of character needed to run a country

For starters, gardening is not about the gardener. It's all about the plants, stupid. Plants may not be able to talk, but they certainly can communicate. Curling or yellowing leaves, brown or rusty spots all point to some serious "infrastructure" issues. Rampant foliage and no fruits or blossoms all indicate that something is out of whack. Neglect such signs of malaise at your peril.

Plants don't care about hype, promises or good intentions. They need cultivation, adequate water and ready access to fertilizers, potash, lime or other resources to keep them healthy and strong. 'Spin' doesn't cut it with plants. Either the gardener delivers or the garden will know and reflect it.

Gardening requires the courage to recognize that balance of power matters. Left to their own devices, invasive species will elbow out their fellows with impunity. A good gardener knows when it's time to intervene and how to keep those pushier plants within bounds in order to benefit the entire garden. Plants need to be free to grow. But greed in a garden is not a good thing. A community full of very aggressive [and misnamed] Obedience Plants leads to a very sad state of affairs.

Good gardeners learn fast that it is unwise to mess with "Mother Nature". Even as I write, the Northern Michigan climate zone in which I garden has shifted 1-2 zones hotter. Cut down a tree and every plant in the garden is going to feel the impact. Weeding doesn't work with a bulldozer. Inefficient watering systems or poor choice of plants for a dry climate zone waste money and resources. The best gardeners are patient and faithful stewards of the earth who take into account the fragility of the ground entrusted to them.

Gardening is hard, hands-on work, an exercise in good leadership. Above all, good gardeners need vision and skills to make the precarious balance of life in a garden successful and sustainable.

Public service in today's world demands the same kind of foresight and wisdom. Come November, as we head for the polls, "thinking green" takes on a whole new urgency and meaning.

CRUNCH TIME

First published in August, 2008

The growing season is five weeks late this year, which means soon a whole bunch of plants (that normally never bloom together) are going to be flowering at the same time. A Master Gardener friend calls this "compacting".

I have come to think of retirement that way. Time is short and precious. Whatever we do, whatever our passion—writing, painting, working in wood, even creating beautiful gardens—our days are finite. And whatever our story, only we can tell or write it.

It is no accident that some artists find themselves producing their best works in the compacted growing season toward the end of their lives. A lot of living, loss and heartache as well as joy, provide the rich soil from which come the late works of a Robert Frost, Rembrandt or others.

Season after season, gardens teach us that spring in all its wild and exuberant beauty is not the final word. Beyond the wild reds and pinks of the summer garden lies another whole palette of royal purples and burnished gold. In the face of winter, fall's prairie asters and mums raise their faces defiantly to the sun.

Never Too Old to Grow

A friend who works in the senior care industry recently told me of a motivational speaker who continues to remind both nursing home residents and staff that the surest way to stay alert and aware even into one's nineties and beyond, is to learn something new—to grow, to flower. Never give up, whatever weather or other conditions may threaten to stunt or diminish our lives. Good advice for any time or age.

Nobody ever says aging is easy. In the face of a potentially disabling medical mis-diagnosis, my 92-year-old mother first mourned—then joined a gym and began to search for ways to flower in spite of her health challenges. Another friend in her eighties makes the weekly climb into the choir loft, despite severe arthritis, to add her voice to a women's choral group that together tackles a repertoire none of them alone in their younger years had dared attempt.

Like plants in a garden, we are not alone planted out there in the bed. With all that support around us, let the growing and budding and blooming begin! And for those of us facing a "compacted" growing season—whether it be as a result of age or health—may that flowering become all the more glorious.

HERE'S TO DO-OVERS

First published in July, 2011

They say in life there are no do-overs. In a garden, that rule doesn't apply. To experience the seasons repeating themselves is an incredible gift in so many ways. It is a mirror held up to our own lives.

Predicting how the seasons in a garden will play out is an exercise in futility. Growing up in Wisconsin, I was never much of a spring person because more often than not, the season lasted a week, tops. Then temperatures would spike in the nineties and all those wonderful bulbs and trees would bloom out overnight. Living in New York, I found that by comparison spring starts early and lasts for months. And then we would arrive in Michigan in June and find the lilacs and other spring favorites still in full flower. It felt like carrying a perpetual spring in our hearts.

So, whatever our location, gardening teaches resilience. If we plant something in an unfortunate location at the end of one season, another year brings with it a chance to try again. Digging out and moving a patch of sunburned hostas both humbles and reassures. We can't always anticipate where problems come, but we can learn the capacity to revisit our choices and move on.

Gardeners also quickly discover the necessity of forgiveness. The Obedient Plant may annoy us with its attempts to take over everything around it. Rarely is it a wise reaction to root the thing out for good. Instead, we might relocate the aggressor next to a hardier plant like Siberian Iris. Or as gardeners, we simply must rise to the challenge and work harder to keep that invasive species in bounds.

Sometimes, sadly, a favorite succumbs to a bad winter—but in those moments, we come face to face with the gift of patience. So-called Daisy Hill I help tend every summer is at the heart of the community garden. I cannot count how often we nearly lost it to frosts, ground swept bare of snow, and most recently, a Bishop Weed invasion. We planted hardier species, tried snow fencing, wrapped the entire hill in plastic for a season to wipe out the weed. We even transplanted survivors, a solitary plug at a time, to fill in the holes. And slowly, the Hill is coming back.

Where there is life, there is struggle, which makes every victory all the more special. Gardening is therapeutic in part because it not only invites but demands second chances. Cultivating that kind of living is something that can transform not a garden or a life, but a world.

Goat's Beard is a deceptively ordinary name for this beauty standing tall in the Bay View Memorial Garden, Michigan.

First published in March, 2009

Last summer my husband, a professional photographer, was game when I asked him to come up with some portraits of our community garden crew at work along Little Traverse Bay one Saturday. As he looked through the viewfinder, the results were not what he expected. There we were, two dozen of us, in poses that defied gravity, all backsides and very few faces in sight. Occupational hazard, I told him.

Well, it's that time of year again. If I google "garden" and "exercise", I find both web sites on gardening *as* exercise and ones on exercise *for* gardeners. And yes, there is a difference.

I personally discovered the distinction the hard way last season. It began when my too enthusiastic spring raking led to a case of tennis elbow that still flares up occasionally. Then my first Saturday back on the community garden crew, I was so excited to be renewing old friendships with both plants and people that I weeded for an hour-and-a-half straight.

Big mistake. I tried to stand up and promptly fell to my knees with a terrible bout of sciatica. While my fellow gardeners commiserated, I crawled over to a bench and lay there. Finally, I managed to limp home. A solid week of stretching and heating pads later, I was able to rejoin the crew. Only this time I got smart and dead-headed, avoiding major bending and kneeling until I got in better shape!

An Ounce of Prevention

According to Gardenfitness.com, experts say that gardening can involve as much stretching, bending, muscle and aerobic exertion as activities like walking and cycling. Regular 35-40 minutes of gardening per day can help joints and muscles remain flexible, as well as stave off diabetes and high blood pressure.

Every year cover stories on the countdown to summer beach time offer blitz plans to get fit before climbing into our swimming togs. Gardenfitness.com lays out a 6-week regimen for the gardener instead, starting each session with a 5-minute stroll through your garden to warm up. My favorites are "flower pot" lifts, much more fun and to the point than hefting barbells. But of course, consult a doctor first.

With the summer garden in its prime, the urge to get out there and dig is irresistible. *Easy does it*, I remind myself. A repeat of last summer's fiasco is definitely not something I intend to schedule on my seasonal gardening calendar!

71

The Memorial Garden crew at work makes me think of
the German nursery rhyme about ducks foraging along
with heads in the water, derrieres in the air.

August

Galliarda aka Blanket Flower thrives as a dramatic
reminder of America's pioneer days in gardens from the
Upper Midwest to Arizona.

KEEP ON KEEPIN' ON

First published in August, 2009

It has been a summer of rain and unseasonable cold. The fall-like nights make us wonder why we made the effort to install those window air conditioners in June. Late but glorious nonetheless, we see the garden bursting into exuberant bloom.

Have the colors ever seemed that bright, that vivid? I think the splendor of those daisies and lilies, the roses with their elegant faces turned upward to the sun, has something to do with all that lush, monsoon-induced greenery around it.

For everything there is a season. Almanacs and weather forecasts do their best to help us anticipate what in the end is unpredictable. But the real miracle—even in a summer of inhospitable "records" and "firsts"—is that life in the garden goes on. Defying the unexpected, the garden adapts and struggles to do what it is meant to do, to bring joy to the beholder.

One of my favorite spring bulbs, the narcissus, draws its name from the mythical character that has become emblematic of our greed-is-good times. Narcissistic super-stars preen and live to excess, forgetful of or oblivious to what thrust them into the public eye in the first place. Instant celebrity is pervasive, as close at hand as our TV remotes.

In Praise of Humility

Gardens don't operate that way. Even the most lushly spectacular of hybrids lives out its singular flowering in the context of a greater whole—the service of the greater good. In a garden, being and doing don't require major soul-searching. Plants strive against all odds to flower. And by definition, they do it together. The result is beautiful.

Simplicity is not as simple as it seems. Plants need care, water and nutrients—and yes, their fair share of sun. They require time, some of them more than a single season before they begin to reach their full potential. Some of that is the gardener's doing. In the end, the plants do their part, an instinct to grow embedded in their very DNA. And when the more invasive get out of hand, the gardener had better intervene.

I am grateful in my dry spells and on overcast days to draw on the memory of my gardens, past and present. The power of that image grows with every new season—in spite and because of me. And as I fret over the blight on the leaves or the mold that suddenly cropped up on the mulch, every bud and flower urges me to persist, hold on. Better days are coming.

Bees love the fragrant lavender border along the sun-drenched paths of the Bay View Memorial Garden, Michigan.

MEDITATION WITH SWEAT

First Published in August, 2010

One definition of gardening: *meditation with sweat.* The blog that came up with that tidbit may be defunct. But the thought is worth preserving. Not just gerontologists but most doctors and psychiatrists agree. Time in a garden—working hard or simply enjoying the experience—is one of the best therapies for our mental health.

Connection to the earth acts like a powerful magnet on the human spirit and psyche. We feel part of forces larger than ourselves. It is hard to be lonely or self-centered in a garden. And gardening engages all the senses: touch, hearing, sight, smell and taste.

Something about plants invite our hands to reach out and touch. We feel a subtle kinship with the leaves and stems brushing at our feet and ankles. Folk wisdom says if we listen closely, we can hear the garden growing. The breath of the wind stirs the buds and blossoms. Our heartbeat steadies at the feast for the eyes spread out before us. Spring's greens foretell rebirth. Summer's lush palette shows us the garden in its prime. Fall's subdued golds and purples calm us in the face of our own mortality.

After the rain last weekend, I balked at weeding out a random mint that had strayed into a bed of astilbe. The distinct herbal scent wafted over the bed, a subtle reminder that smell is the first of the senses we recognize at birth and the last we experience before death. I couldn't resist. I tasted a leaf. Even veggie-haters marvel that carrots or pole beans taste so much better right from the plant than on a plate.

Encountering the Holy

It seems no accident that sacred books, in many religious traditions, picture the Divinity walking with humankind in a garden. Stories of Allah and the Creator God in the Old and New Testament contain such imagery. Meditating Buddhas are among the most popular garden statuary. One retail search engine boasts 4,000-plus Buddha bird feeders online. Sadly, I had to leave behind the lovely Saint Francis in one of my New York pocket gardens when we moved. But after a decade in that spot, it belonged there as surely the plants around it.

Meditation with sweat. Like a lot of other gardeners, I am guilty of talking about 'working' in a garden. What an odd word for something we so dearly love. Instead, it might be more fitting, life-transforming, to rethink our time spent in the garden as a subtle, unspoken prayer.

76

It was my grandmother's favorite flower. Bachelor Button conjures up precious memories in the Bay View Memorial Garden, Michigan.

Hollyhocks stand as sentinels in the sandy soil and summer sunlight of Petoskey, Michigan.

VARIETY IS THE SPICE

First published in July, 2013 - May, 2013

Want to teach your children to treasure diversity in a global world? Then get out there in the mud and garden. Gardens model a healthy vision of community better than most. If we want everybody and everything in life to be just like us, then metaphorically speaking it makes sense to plant a lawn and be done with it. Drop gardeners into that environment and they will be very unhappy campers.

Lawns all look alike. The lone neighbor who loves dandelions or seeds wildflowers into the grass is not apt to be popular on the block. Folks with gardens in their heart don't fear diversity, they cultivate it. Even if a garden boasts all hostas or roses, the challenge becomes to see how many different kinds can thrive in a given spot. A so-called "bridal garden" may be white, but that doesn't mean the plants are identical, too.

It is all but impossible to rub elbows with that kind of aesthetic and not carry it over into one's personal life. The American Community Gardening Association, says a Michigan State University Extension website, celebrates the belief that gardening together promotes diversity and empowers people to "share their expertise, their cultures, ideas and feelings in addition to passing on skills to one another."

And if a plant decides to crowd out everything that isn't just like them? Then it's up to the gardener to take the lead and make it safe for those other plants to thrive and grow.

Modern society often has been criticized for denying the realities of aging and death. There can be something unhealthy about idealizing perpetual youth. But even gardening, perhaps the ultimate reality check, constantly wrestles with the delicate issue of balance.

As a volunteer for a memorial garden in Michigan every summer, I find it spiritually challenging to be part of a team that works hard to maintain the plantings so that visitors see only the *Eternal*. Whenever a flower is past its peak, we deadhead it. Damaged foliage is removed as quickly and unobtrusively as possible. Only life survives.

Gardeners know only too well that nothing lasts. And yet, those precious roses of summer remain perfect in memory long after the ground is covered once again in a vast sheet of glistening white.

Fall is coming soon. *Carpe diem*, the garden reminds us. Love, laugh and cultivate the art of living while we can. Time is the ultimate gift to use wisely or squander. It is the precious soil in which we grow.

TRANSPLANT SHOCK
First published in October, 2010

Depressed about the future? Plant something. Gardeners have faith in tomorrow. Plants know all about change. Through it all, gardening can both ground us and give us the courage to keep reinventing ourselves, over and over again.

My own career path was never obvious. After grad school in Wisconsin, I went to work for the university's publishing house. On weekends, my sanity factor was prowling the Wisconsin woods with a wildflower book in hand. I still have it, ragged now. My inked dates next to the line drawings still record when I first spotted a plant. To this day, I still pen in details of such encounters on my Midwest visits.

Publishing houses were non-existent in the tiny Michigan town where I settled next. The rural economy was in the pits. After a major struggle as a dislocated homemaker, I found work writing and teaching school kids about career opportunities and their unemployed parents about the job hunting process. All the while, I personally sought refuge in tending my Rubber Plants and Jade Trees.

One Challenging Transplant after the Other

Moving on, we headed East to New York and then Pennsylvania, where I worked as a consultant for the U.S. Labor Department, wrote a syndicated column on work and grants that landed me jobs as administrator of a county economic development agency, a chaplain and music school marketing director. Plants eased the transition. I hit the toll booths en route with a veritable jungle in the back of our van. Later in Iowa, I worked as a career counselor and researcher with a rural think tank. After hours, with spade and shears, I turned the overgrown gardens around the house in which I found myself into a perennial show garden.

In a transition to so-called retirement on Long Island, I worked as a church music director by day and novelist at night. My personal garden and summer community garden experience in Michigan grounded me anew as I redefined what it meant to be a survivor.

Plants do what they do. They search for whatever allows them to grow, like my intrepid Ajuga traveling three feet along the driveway to find the sun. I admire such tenacity. How did "pinks" land behind our Michigan cottage? I didn't plant them. They are beautiful all the same.

Life like gardens can have the power to surprise us. We just need to adapt and keep growing and planting for the future, no matter what.

September

Fall Thistle, like a plant with a bad hair day, dots the landscape in Northern Michigan.

LABOR DAY
First published in September, 2013

Labor Day might be a bizarre time to write about *recreation*. But as gardeners, that mix of work and play is at the heart and soul of why we love what we do. Gardening is both about creation and re-creation, about struggle and joy. In the garden, seeming opposites go hand and hand to build a lifestyle that can not only enrich but sustain us. All good stuff.

As a child, I discovered that my parents took their 'play' very seriously. Whether a week or ten days or two weeks, we always traveled together as a family. And while dragging ourselves out of bed during the work and school week was not always easy, on vacation we were up with the birds, hiking and sightseeing and learning intensely to appreciate the world around us. I owe my parents an enormous debt for those habits.

"I don't work like crazy all year," Mom always said, "to sleep it away." A person can cram a lot of living even into a long weekend.

No Retirement from Living

Science and medicine are discovering that a healthy attitude toward *recreation* is one of the factors that contributes to long and happy lives. On our worst days, we may fantasize about lying in a puddle as the ideal way to recover from life's strains and stress. In fact, says research psychologist Leslie Martin, co-author of the new book *The Longevity Project*, "those who worked the hardest tended to live the longest".

Who knew? After hearing for years that it was time to 'chill out', stop worrying and relax, we discover that hard work, caring and focus and discipline is really good for us after all.

The key, psychologist Martin says, is *consistency*. A healthy physical life is not dependent upon how hard we work out, but finding something that keeps us moving on a regular basis. One of the specific activities Martin recommends is gardening.

For those of us who spent our early years as nerds, it's time to get up and off the couch. Plants that become root-bound will ultimately fare poorly or even die. And for a plant to retire from life is not an option. As a goal, 'retirement' is not guaranteed to bring human beings fulfillment or happiness. At whatever age, life is meant to be lived, purposefully and with energy. It is how we—and plants—are made.

Labor Day and gardening celebrate the same precious insight. We are truly fortunate when work and play become all but inseparable. In our gardens, in our day jobs—and yes, in retirement.

Red Hot Poker aka Torch Flower [Kniphofia]
blazes in a Northern Michigan garden.

A sunflower, nature's sundial, lifts its face to the heavens in Northern Michigan farm near Petoskey, Michigan.

LET'S HEAR IT FOR FLOWERS !

First published in September, 2012

As a garden writer, on the speaking circuit I often ask audiences why they garden. More often than not, from guys anyway, the response I get is: if I can't eat it, I don't grow it. All the more reason why I was pleasantly surprised when at a children's workshop at the Petoskey, Michigan library, I got a very, very different response.

A young boy, a fourth grader if I recall, piped right up and said, "Flowers. I like growing flowers." Astonished, I asked the reason. "Because they make things more beautiful," he said.

It doesn't get a whole lot better than that. Turns out, the young man learned that love of the gloriously impractical from gardening with his grandmother. And oh how much poorer our lives would be without that capacity for whimsy.

An article in the weekend *Parade* supplement once featured a fascinating article on gardening with children, especially the role gardens can play in teaching kids about community. While I whole-heartedly agree, the piece—like so many others on gardening with children—was all about growing veggies. But for me the young man in the library was precious proof that the notion of aesthetics or beauty for its own sake is not uniquely an adult concept.

In the garden, kids can cultivate an appreciation for beauty that surpasses the so-called necessities of life. Sometimes it is enough just to make things beautiful. Through the primitive cave paintings in France and Spain, even our earliest ancestors left behind an artistic commentary on their world. In our modern often hard-headed, buy-and-sell world, where arts programs are often axed right and left when times get tough, what a fantastic goal for anyone to make their own: to promote beauty for its own sake. On that score, the garden can be a powerful teacher.

Gardens do not have the staying power of art on rock walls, hidden away over the centuries. But the very fleeting nature of a garden's presence among us, season after season, is a powerful commentary on the ephemeral quality of life. The enduring hardscape of life is important. So is the memory created by a pot garden on a patio, tended with love.

The young man's favorite plant proved to be sunflowers. A great choice. Sometimes the old tried and true may, indeed, be the best. We have a month-and-change before we lose that beauty in the garden for the season. Enjoy it, my friends and fellow gardeners, while we can.

SURVIVOR TREE

First Published in November, 2012

Fall is in its final flower. Change is in the air. After a decade-and-a-half 'wintering' in New York, the countdown has begun. By the time this column runs, the movers will have shown up at our Long Island home for the trek West.

With much of our lives here already stowed in boxes, in our final week we decided on one last fling in "the City", the place that has been such an enormous part of our time in New York. Our long weekend became crammed with revisiting some of our favorite haunts. We wandered the brownstone-lined streets, took in the bustle of Times Square. After a Broadway matinee, we hung out at the stage door—something we had never done before—as star-struck as any groupie around.

And on that crisp Saturday morning, our pilgrimage also took us south to the very tip of Manhattan to the newly dedicated 9-11 Memorial. Although we had continued our regular visits to the City after those tragic events, we had drawn the line at visiting the World Trade Center site itself. Images were unavoidable in the media, but the human anguish of those times had engraved itself painfully in our hearts.

Now, through a flood of memories, we sensed the architects of the Memorial had indeed 'gotten it right'. Thousands of arching streams of water flowed together into the basins, a collective expression of a nation's grief and affirmation of the human melting pot of the City itself. How small the pools seemed as measures of the footprint of those Twin Towers.

A forest of swamp oaks, grassy lawns and ivy lined the pathways. And off to one side, unmarked but unmistakable, stood the so-called Survivor Tree. When the original crews of volunteers at the site first found the Callery pear, it had been reduced to an eight-foot stump. Lovingly, the trunk and roots were moved north to Central Park in an attempt to revive the decimated tree.

Seasons passed. With time and care, the branches regrew, as if from a graft. Its crown stretched to over 20 feet before tragedy struck yet again. In a severe storm that wiped out thousands of New York's venerable trees, the Survivor Tree too found itself violently uprooted.

Loving hands once again went to work. And before the Memorial opened, the Survivor Tree that would not die was returned to the original site. Still secured with transplant wires, it stands a silent witness to the power of hope and perseverance. Where one might least expect it, surrounded by towering steel and glass, once again we are surprised and humbled by a life-lesson from the garden.

"You have your column for the month," my husband said as we stood together in the tree's shadow. Yes, I thought—and far more than that, whatever comes.

Daisy Hill is the author's favorite spot in the Bay View Memorial Garden, Michigan—a sea of white against the intense blue waters of Little Traverse Bay.

BEAUTY OF THE DOWN-TIMES

First published in September, 2009

Regardless of the climate zone in which we garden, we are bound to confront those seasonal 'fallow' times which defy easy solutions. Spring bulbs have died out and it is too early for the iris and lilies. Mid-summer is past its peak and the mums and prairie asters are still only in bud.

It is so tempting to resort to a 'quick fix' and use annuals mixed among the perennials to solve those transition problems. Species like impatiens just keep going and going and going, from early summer to the first frost. But clever gardeners also can learn to cultivate the beauty of green-on-green during such seasonal transitions. Even without flowers in bloom, leaf textures and shapes catch our attention in a garden.

Shade-loving hostas are good examples of this. Gardeners actually deadhead hosta flowers early-on to send maximum nutrients to the large and amazing varied leaves. Not until late in the season are those elegant flower stalks allowed to blossom freely. Unique and attractive, astilbe, day lily and peony foliage holds up well until early fall.

Flowers past their peak can also be rich additions to the garden's palette. Feathery borders of lavender attracts the eye even as the colors move from a rich purple to a monochrome gray-green. Allium blooms are spectacular long after they have dried in place. Astilbe flowers fade so subtly that it is difficult often to tell when they are in bud or bloomed out.

Gardeners know they have done a great job when they squint at the 'fallow' garden and still see dynamic motion and color even without the more obvious reds, yellows and purples to draw the eye. Like a fine black and white photograph, careful use of shape and structure can appeal as powerfully to our senses as a color print. One thing I love about early spring are the many shades of green. Leaves can create an amazingly varied landscape, long before flowering plants come into their own.

Subtleties of garden design can teach us a lot about weathering transitions and changes in our own lives. 'In between' seasons can be blessings in disguise, challenging us to rethink the shifting ground upon which we stand. Forget grand gestures. Barren down-times that follow life's dramatic disappointments and losses sometimes work to bring out strengths of soul and character we never knew existed.

As the philosopher of all things childhood, Kermit the Frog reminds us all: to think 'green' is not always easy. But life's monochrome moments can also result in beauty we never ever imagined possible.

October

Angel's Trumpet [Datura or moonflower] floats like an elegant dancer in a Wisconsin garden. The plant is no angel. If ingested, all parts of this beauty are poisonous.

AUTUMN JOY

First published in October, 2013

"Do not go gentle into that good night," the Welsh poet Dylan Thomas said. He could have been writing about the garden's final flowering.

Fall in the garden is my favorite time of year. The shadows seem longer, the light more intense. The pastels of spring and the wild palette of summer give way to solemn tones. Goldenrod spreads molten light over the meadows. Field asters stand watch in purple liver. A silver-tinged sea of grasses stirs in the rising wind.

As I pass the farm stands, the mums are in their prime—glorious mounds of orange, crimson, lilac and butter yellow. No matter how hardy a mum's label, my luck with them over the years has been spotty. And successful fall gardening is about survival.

Perhaps more than any other perennial, Autumn Joy Sedum has proven true to its name. The vibrant rusty red flower-heads glow brightly long after those more finicky mums of mine have called it a day. And even then, the garden is rewarded with a kind of second flowering. Sedum's dried, chestnut-hued seed heads stand sentinel alone even as the first frost tinges the grass and the first dusting of snow begins to fall.

Soon enough, only bare limbs and dry stubble remain. The growing season is over. The wrack of the garden is complete. Laying it to rest becomes a solemn business. Fall's calendar is unforgiving. Avoidance and delay putting the garden to bed only leads to freezing hands and struggles with rock-hard ground.

"Kind surgeons leave stinking wounds," a Dutch proverb warns. Buried under all that waste and plant debris, the garden of the future could not hope to thrive. My last farewell to the garden becomes a frenzy of pruning and clipping, blistered hands clearing away the old and the spent.

Mission accomplished. As a gardener I feel a strange sense of peace, a renewed clarity that moves me to another place entirely. With plants reduced to isolated mounds and clumps, the shape of the garden becomes more transparent. *This*, I say, is my garden as it is intended to be!

I can't linger long. The first hard frost waits for no one. I lay down fresh mulch to secure the future for the more vulnerable of the perennials. For good measure, with bulb planter in hand, I dig in a half-bushel of bulbs, an investment of hope in the spring to come.

There are life lessons in such transitions. One growing season is ending. Another has begun.

Last roses of the season huddle against a picket fence in Greenport, a historic fishing village on Long Island's North Shore, New York.

DIRT THERAPY

First published in October, 2009

I came across an ad for heirloom.com on the internet the other day that talked about gardening as "dirt therapy". I had to smile—even as I struggle with the aftermath of three brutal days of year-end garden clean-up. Non-stop aches and pains. My broken, utterly disgusting finger nails.

Dirt therapy. How lucky those of us are to have experienced it. Getting out there and working (and playing) in the mud can do more for mental health than a bucket load of pills or hours of counseling sessions. And the price is right, as cheap as a lowly seed packet, clippers and trowel.

If we are looking for the ultimate reality-check in an often shallow and greed-obsessed world, gardening reminds us what really matters. Whether we tend a veggie patch or a stunning bed of flowers, a garden pulls us up short and reminds us how beautiful, how short and finite life is. We learn to embrace the rhythms of life and death. And it is no small thing to learn when to stand and fight in the face of life's challenges. Or when it is time to deadhead, cut our losses and move on.

Putting Down Roots

In a garden, age counts. Quick fixes are few and far between. Perennials often take a year or two before they truly bloom flat-out where they've been planted. I feel every year as the dirt accumulates on my tired hands and feet. There are times as a gardener I also feel wonderfully like a kid again, wading through puddles in a warm spring rain.

Gardens demand putting down roots. They are about sharing, about building relationships and healthy communities. The garden becomes the ultimate democracy where every plant has its worth, deserves to be cherished and protected. The rules of the road apply not just to the weak or powerless, but to every green thing growing. In that world, the gardener's job—to nurture and, yes, referee—becomes a privilege, a sacred trust.

Even as another gardening season draws to a close, I give thanks for the cycle of nurturing that draws me closer to the earth and my inner self. My plants depend on me and I on them for a shared vision of the beautiful. Ours is a companionship as old as humankind's first farmer who ceased to forage and planted a seed.

So even as I drag out the heating pad to write this column, I give thanks for the *dirt therapy* that put me in this shape. Life lessons from the garden come in many forms and guises.

The author and one of her granddaughters
go after the weeds together one Saturday morning on
the Bay View Memorial Garden crew.

Plants do not depend on color alone to catch our eye. The patterns on the petals of these Pinks aka Dianthus provide a touch of drama in the author's northern Michigan garden.

First published in October, 2008

Willard Scott on the Today show once featured a couple, married happily for seventy-five years. The secret of their longevity? Never fight. When it gets a bit tense on the home front, the husband goes out and gardens. Both say they have the biggest garden on the block.

I laughed. But truth is, gardening as therapy and healer makes an awful lot of sense. I have told friends for years that, for me, the less glamorous tasks like weeding and deadheading have all the satisfaction of cleaning the bathroom but none of the drawbacks. A guy gets outside in the fresh air. It is obvious that something tangible has been accomplished. All of it good.

Not surprising, most gardeners love to talk about the deeper meaning of their favorite past-time. There are web sites galore devoted to quotes about gardening's balm for the human psyche. For starters, gardening *grounds* us. Note the language!

Poetically among gardeners, the tough fall clean-up is known as *putting the garden to bed.* I can't imagine a kinder, gentler way of describing that bittersweet moment when we realize it's time to call it quits for the season. With the tough task behind us, visions of *long winter naps* and the promise of spring's *awakening* are there to sustain us.

Then there's my personal favorite gardening job and expression, *deadheading.* It took some imagination to come up with the whimsical term for eliminating bloomed-out and unsightly plant growth. Decapitating would have been another possibility. But then deadheading's goal is not loss or destruction, but encouraging new growth.

What's in a name? According to the "Ask Oxford" online dictionary, the word 'garden' itself stems from 14th century Northern French *gardin*—a variation of Old French *jardin* (still used in modern French). Both *garden* and the word *yard* also have roots in the older Germanic word *geard* which means 'building, home, region'. These are among the oldest words in the English language. Names of Russian cities with similar roots, like Novgorod and Petrograd, trace back to words for 'enclosures' and secure spaces. Over time, yard and garden become linked linguistically to safety and home. I like that notion.

Gardeners need shears and all sorts of other sharp objects lying around. Predators and muscle strains abound. Yet gardens also can be wonderful places of safety and shelter for both gardeners and plants alike.

95

MISSION ACCOMPLISHED

First published in October, 2007

In the autumn of my life, more and more I am coming to appreciate that year-end ritual of taking down the garden. Letting a garden sit in ruins at the end of the season is not healthy for the plants or the ground. A gardener who avoids putting a garden to bed misses a precious opportunity to learn about not just plants, but themselves.

An untended fall garden creates a breeding ground for mold, fungus and viruses that can destroy next season's growth at its root. Even knowing that, taking down a garden demands courage.

In the community garden where I volunteer every summer, the master gardener tags the bushes to be spared in advance. The crew then hand-cuts the hydrangeas and stalks of the oriental lilies so that in the carnage to come, the bulbs and roots will not be yanked out accidentally. Then come the weed-whackers, mowing everything down to within six inches of the ground.

Mourning Our Losses

It hurts to see all that former splendor go. The mouse that called the hosta 'home' now has nowhere to go. Even weeds can't hide. With the last of the foliage raked and carried off, the crew takes one last shot at rooting out the dandelions, bind weed and wild mustard that eluded our trowels all summer.

The decision is made to leave the late-blooming sedum stand at the height of its russet glory. No one wants to deny that lone sentinel its last flowering. Even dried and wind-torn when the snows come, it still speaks to all passersby: *A garden once was here. Spring is coming.*

Our life journey isn't much different. It is never easy to let go of worn out dreams, the worries and baggage of seasons past. Gardens remind us why it must be done from time to time: to free ourselves for new life—determined and thorough, without false sentimentality.

Nothing can eradicate the memory of our garden at its peak, vibrant and strong. But living, growing things need their resting season, too. Fallow time is not about death but new life to come. That fallow time is both precious and necessary. Nurturing that fallow period is part and parcel of the gardener's creed. *Simplify. Think ahead.*

For everything there is a season. As the earth sleeps, deep in that rich soil, the garden down there is waiting once again for loving hands to tend and nurture and admire it. It will flower once again.

96

An elegant rose unfolds to the morning sun in the Bay View Memorial Garden, Michigan.

POETRY OF THE GARDEN
First published in October, 2014

Almanacs say winter once again may come hard and stay long. The earth is resting, something we all can understand. So once our houseplants are duly watered, we gardener types often turn to books and catalogs to keep us going until another growing season begins.

On the literary front, I highly recommend a poem by Robert Browning, "Abt Vogler" to help put that long time of waiting into beautiful perspective. Although written about an organist and not a gardener, the emotions expressed in the poem are ones that every gardener can understand. Like performing a piece of music, gardening is an ephemeral art. Beauty fades with the flower, lives on only in memory. That spiritual truth challenges the winter gardener to treasure time and the coming season as never before.

Prophets describe the human journey as a cycle from dust to dust. Like flowers in the field, we have but brief moments in the sun. Such images resonate especially at this time of year, as we mourn the end of the gardening season.

But when we gardeners shed shoes and gloves, we find time to reflect on gardening's intimate connection to our spiritual lives. One of the most powerful sacred encounters in the Judeo-Christian tradition comes from the ancient text known as Exodus. From within the heart of a burning bush, a voice commands Moses, then a bewildered shepherd on Mount Horeb, to remove his shoes in the presence of the Holy.

There is a perpetual life-lesson for gardeners in that story. Many of us gardener folk experience childlike joy at playing in the mud. That intimate, unvarnished connection to the dirt under our feet and finger nails also serves to 'ground' us. Now is not forever. The art of living demands we honor that truth with reverence and ever-renewed intensity. For everything there is a season.

October is a time of endings. The sedate and regal fall landscape with its purples, crimson and gold fade to a darker palette. Rain heightens the smell of decaying leaves underfoot. Random at first, hoar frost coats the branches in rare and exquisite crystals that melt with the sun. The earth grows cold and hard underfoot.

Depressing, perhaps. Right now the exuberant greens of May seem a lifetime away. But in this quiet season of turning inward lie the seeds of new growth. So it is with the garden. With our lives.

November

Asters and Sedum huddle together in the author's
fall garden in Southold, Long Island, New York.

CULTIVATING PRIDE OF PLACE
First published in November, 2009

A reader's provocative letter started me thinking about how obsessive-compulsive and short-sighted our society can be. She wrote:

> *Recently my apartment complex sent out a newsletter telling all tenants that it's fall and time to get rid of all our flowers and clean off our patios and porches. I was so upset. I spend lots of $$ making sure I have a variety of blooms that will last not only for summer, but into the fall, until frost. I'm not a expert gardener, but I love the beauty of growing things. WHATEVER HAPPENED TO COMMUNITY GARDENING?*

I fully appreciate her situation. As we got older, my spouse and I thought about moving into a condo or apartment. The prospect of giving up our back-breaking but precious plots of perennials was a serious deterrent.

Some housing complex managers seem to get very hyper as winter approaches. Frozen stubble standing on tenant patios certainly is not very attractive. But random date-driven policies that rush the season don't seem to be a good solution either.

My mother faced a related problem in her condo association. A few owners insisted that uniform bushes made the community look more appealing. In fact, mom's dogged efforts to interject a bit of color into her 'yard' did a lot to liven up a cookie-cutter looking neighborhood. Eventually her gardening transformed that whole association.

Cultivating a Sense of Home

Smart facility managers appreciate that well-tended annuals and perennials communicate an environment of warmth and community pride. *Here*, they say to potential renters or owners, *you can feel truly at home.*

In a similar vein, garden statuary and flamboyant plantings in communal housing can get out of hand. But there has to be a way to deal with potential problems rather than just saying, No. Overly formal or sterile landscapes have all the appeal of an Addam's family cartoon!

To arrange a meeting with the building manager might lead to positive change. Expert gardener or not, we can offer to organize a community garden team that helps advise folks what to plant—ideas that will stretch the blooming season around the building as long as possible. It is certainly an atmosphere worth cultivating.

100

Late-flowering daisy mums are popular favorites in this Long Island, New York farm stand.

THANKSGIVING DAY
First published in December, 2008

Sing a song of harvest home, the traditional Thanksgiving hymn happily encourages us. Safely squirreled away in the freezer, the fruits of a summer of vegetable gardening reward us with memories of work productively done. The garden sleeps. Now is the time for family and friendships and a well-deserved fallow time for the gardener as well. Winter is coming.

In my novel, *Time in a Garden*, the heroine and gardener Eve writes a great deal about gardening and growing older, about life beautifully lived. "Words like 'risk' and 'hope' and 'grace' do not pop up a lot in horticultural magazines," she says, "That is odd, because you cannot survive long in the gardening business without them."

Hope is a commodity we all badly need these days, in and out of the garden. "As a culture," Eve writes in her diary, "we tend to want immediate gratification. Gardens do not operate that way. Gardening works only when we learn to plant by a calendar in which months and years and even generations become the measure of what has been accomplished."

Shortcuts and greed-is-good ethics don't work particularly well in the garden. If we get lazy and plant the bulbs too shallow, they freeze or rot. If we skimp on fertilizer or don't keep an eye on the nitrogen content of the soil, the harvest is skimpy or we wind up with great foliage and no veggies. In the end, all the alpha-dog hubris in the world cannot substitute for honest and careful stewardship.

For good or ill in a garden, we reap what we sow. Yet, for all our short-sightedness, our gardens also remind us it is never too late to begin again. "Gardening opens the possibility of second chances," Eve writes. "Our failures are only final if we give up or if we refuse to learn from our experiences. The saga of a gardener is the story of hope."

"Gardening is both life-affirming and humbling. It teaches us to have faith in new life to come and to hold on through the darker days. It grounds us—literally and figuratively—in what really matters as the seasons play out around us."

The greatest gifts we can share with our families this holiday season are not bought with mega-bucks, but with love—a life-lesson that an investment in gardening can give. Seed packets and garden tools won't break the bank. But the dividends they pay are priceless.

Where have all the lilies gone? These spectacular
beauties that graced the Bay View Memorial Garden in
Northern Michigan flower. As winter approaches, they
bloom only in memory.

First published in December, 2010

Our holiday gifts come when and how we least expect them. My last official gardening act for the season was to dig in seven enormous pots of sedum. I had coveted those sturdy perennials all fall, a fiery blaze on the makeshift wooden racks in front of the grocery. *Autumn Joy*, the labels said. When the sales sticker hit a buck-fifty a pot, I couldn't resist any longer, even though the plants appeared to be half dead.

Buyer's remorse hit as the clerk tallied up the bill. The once stunning flower heads were a dried out, nondescript rust. At the plant's base, cabbage-like new growth had begun to establish itself. Even as I dug away at the hardening soil to plant them, I kept telling myself not to get my hopes up.

In another week I couldn't have gotten my shovel in the ground. The wind was howling out of the north. I had to chase the now-empty pots as they rolled down the driveway. Still, at that price, I couldn't be too choosy about the survival rate over the winter.

There's no accounting for my obsession with last-rose-of-summer plant rescue operations. If I'm lucky, I manage to save one in three. In graduate school, finances were an excuse. Nowadays, nursery owners just roll their eyes as I forage through their Clearance tables. I tell myself that somebody has to love the poor overstock salvia nobody else wanted.

"You're a tough one," a manager told me last summer after I spent a good half hour sorting through the spring rejects. *A softy*, actually. But I didn't argue.

Cut back the stems, a voice in my head told me. Let all the energy go to the roots. A couple weeks ago, I might have been tempted to leave the extravagant red sedum blossoms finish out their blooming season. Aesthetics can distract a gardener from the task at hand, which greatly reduces a plant's chances of survival, whatever the season.

Gardening experts tell us that in the long run, insisting on the healthiest possible plant stock is a wise investment. But one look at those sad-looking factory-rejects and logic didn't weigh heavily on the scale. I loaded the cart with pots, including the fold-down wire baby seat. By the time I got home, the car's cargo area was littered with plant residue.

Call it folly or a leap of faith. A sure bet, that bed with the sedum is the first place I check in spring for signs of life. A book-maker wouldn't touch those odds with a ten-foot pole.

A sunbathing frog enjoys one of the last summery late fall days, hanging out in the author's New York pond.

TENDING OUR INNER CHILD

First published in September, 2010

Do you consider yourself a "late bloomer"? Do you talk about "weeding out the deadwood" in your life? Some of the most colorful and common expressions in our language can be traced back to the human fascination with gardens and gardening.

Close to 3 million internet sites collect garden phrases. Among the most popular: *The grass is always greener on the other side of the fence; separating wheat from the chaff; everything's coming up roses; to lead someone up or down the garden path; reaping what we sow; a bird in the hand is worth two in the bush; life isn't always a bed of roses.* We say we're *sitting on the fence* when it comes to making a decision. And we treasure life's plain old 'garden-variety' experiences.

What is about gardens that colors the language of our everyday? Like the proverbial pigs in mud, the prospect of playing in the dirt speaks to the inner child in all of us. My husband grew up in New York City with glass-strewn alleys and open hydrants in the summer heat for his playground. But he still speaks with borderline awe of the tiny patch of immaculate grass his father planted and treasured outside their walk-up apartment. It was his childhood job to trim that grass as needed—with a household shears.

A Midwestern native myself, I was never far from the earth. We filched berries out of gardens along the block and held neighborhood parades waving the stalks and jumbo leaves of rhubarb as flags. Nothing ever tasted quite as good as beans or pea pods right off the plant. I can close my eyes and remember exactly what the mud felt like under my bare toes after a hard summer rain.

Scientists have documented the healing sight of green things growing on the human psyche. Travel agents can testify to the power of fall color tours and the changing of the seasons to ignite our imaginations.

Many of us soon will be agonizing over putting our gardens to bed for the season. Maybe it is time to just stand dead still amid those rows of veggies or beds of perennials and enjoy.

Not just gardeners, but folks who call their thumbs anything but green, set their emotional clocks by the seasons. And ready or not, the smells and sights and sounds of change are in the air all around us. Words alone cannot hope to do them justice.

December

Winterberry adds a stunning splash of holiday color
along the pond of a Long Island, New York tree farm.

ANNUALS AND PERENNIALS
First published in December, 2014

The season of lights in the shadow of winter are upon us. December is a time for celebration and stock-taking, for resolutions that anticipate another growing season. Though right now it seems light-years away. Falling back on the language of the garden can help us cultivate the kind of dreams we have for ourselves.

For starters, are we annuals or perennials. And what does that mean for the months and year ahead?

Annuals don't fear change. Their role is to inject a burst of color into a monochrome world. They're low maintenance and don't obsess over the fragility of life. They simply bloom flat-out, petal to the metal in their one and only growing season, fearless about the future. Annuals may seem reckless, superficial, naive. The fact remains, their passion for life inspires both envy and emulation. They bloom while and where they can.

Perennials are in it for the long haul. They need more tending and TLC, which they reward by returning year after year. Change in the perennials' world is a subtle business as they stretch outward to fill the barren spaces around them. Seeming setbacks like pruning strengthen them in the long run. Perennials are stoic and persistent, steady and predictable. Their tenacity comforts us. Perennials remind us that life is about seasons and cycles. Bad as a season may be, this too shall pass.

The denizens of the plant world are an amazingly diverse lot. Grasses may appear fragile, but they are the masters of resilience. Succulents and cactus prepare for the worst by building up inner resources to weather the droughts that lie ahead. Bulbs and tubers have learned the art of strategic retreat, storing up the energy to flower again.

Appearances can be deceptive. From the ugliest beginnings come some of the most beautiful results. Witness one of my favorites: the iris which blossoms gloriously from those gnarled and very inelegant tubers. Exotically beautiful as the orchid may be, when it comes to fragrance, it cannot compete with far lowlier species in the plant world.

The world of plants teaches us what it means to realize potential and to use gifts whatever the climate. Plants are consummate survivors. We can learn from them all. As the holidays and New Year approach, I cannot imagine greater gifts than ones that make us better, more creative and successful gardeners. The life lessons that come with them? Priceless.

The ultimate evergreen, holly and its brilliant red berries thrive in the author's Long Island, New York garden—a traditional and treasured symbol of the winter holiday season.

SEASON OF THE IMAGINATION
First published in December, 2008

I'm a Sting fan. One of my favorite songs of all-time is his haunting "Fields of Gold"—a lyrical saga about love for life and things growing. Reviews of his album "If on a Winter's Night" describe it as capturing the heart of this 'season of spirits', including a haunting version of the French carol about the Angel Gabriel coming from heaven clad in drifting snow, with eyes a-flame.

Sting talks about these barren months as a time of mystery and storytelling, the "season of the imagination". Landscapes, he says, are "magically" even eerily "transformed by snow."

His poetry truly warms my heart as I watch my own garden going to sleep for the winter. Earth hardens. The chill penetrates deeper and deeper. Snow descends like feathers from a quilt to blanket the land, thick and heavy, encrusted with diamonds.

Out there in that stillness, my garden lives on. Some plant roots still draw nutrients from the seemingly dead ground. Others lie fallow and dormant, waiting for the thaws that will awaken them again. Dried stalks thrust defiantly through the glacial landscape surrounding them, testament to a life well and truly lived, a blooming season past.

If I have a religion, it is music, Sting says, because it speaks to his soul. Obviously, so does the power of the garden. Like music in its many guises, the garden raises us above ourselves, makes us aware of things beyond the fragile bounds of the everyday. The garden speaks to us at our most human.

Courage. Love. Forgiveness. Memory. It is no accident that gardeners have created a whole poetic lexicon surrounding the plants they tend. Shakespeare's Ophelia, in her deep grief and madness, conjures up some of them, in one of the most powerful moments in theatrical literature, ever. "There's rosemary, that's for remembrance; pray you love, remember," she says. And for herself, there's only rue, the herb symbolizing regret.

My only regrets as I watch my sleeping garden is that I didn't take more time to enjoy it. Even with my regular morning and evening walks through those lush and beautiful beds, it seems never to have been enough. Like a labyrinth, a garden is meant to be walked, to be meditated in and upon. A garden is meant to be lived, not just cultivated or visited.

In the long winter ahead, more than ever, the garden is loved.

An ice storm coats the author's New York garden in a glistening sheet of white.

GARDENING FOR LIFE
First published in December, 2011

Our gardens lie in ruins at our feet. Stubble crackles underfoot. Flurries are in the air. We can sense the year's inevitable turning. In such transitional times, the wisdom a garden teaches can arm us for life, better than just about anything I know.

Value the Unexpected. I am continuously amazed when I spot those last tiny blossoms hanging on in one particular bed alongside the house long after the hard frost. That spot never gets enough sun. Everything struggles to grow there. But just when I'm prepared to write it off, for a few precious weeks every year that unlikely late bloomer becomes the final bastion of productivity and beauty in the garden.

Seize Hope in Whatever Unlikely Form It Takes. Just as the ground becomes too hard to till and we fight to dig in that package of bulbs that went lost in the garage earlier in the season, the seed catalogs begin to arrive. The seasonal rhythms in a gardener's world are at once predictable and defy our assumptions about what is permanent and what is not. The ongoing demand that we rethink change in our lives may be one of gardening's most enduring gifts to us.

Embrace Life's Transience. Modern global politics are teaching us a lot about limits. But then my garden taught me that a long time ago. Rain comes, no thanks to us. Sunlight answers to a higher power. Whatever we believe about global warning, drought can put a damper on a garden quicker than just about anything.

Years ago, I started out with such grandiose visions of chewing up the sod in the front yard and planting a cottage garden—a modest foot a year, until sciatica and a case of tennis elbow proved painful reality checks. There are times when our garden tells us loud and clear, *Enough*. It isn't just laziness to leave the rake propped against my back fence every fall and spring. The blasted thing is a daily call to conscience. Whatever grandiose delusions we may cultivate, in the end we are only human. Gardens keep us humble.

Even these early nights and chill days are teachable moments. Late fall and winter can be dismissed as the consummate down-time. But our plants need it. We gardeners need it as well. In a world where workaholism rules, long winter naps can do more for our mental health than a boatload of nutritional supplements. *Well done*, our gardens are telling us. Stop to reflect. Recharge and renew. 'Tis the season.

Time comes alive in this imaginative cactus sundial in the Desert Botanical Garden in Phoenix, Arizona.

CELEBRATING DARKNESS
First published in December, 2007

"You must die a little," the narrator of the classic musical *The Fantastiks* says at the end of the play, "in order to live." The wonderful thing about seasons, winter in particular, is their potential as a wake-up call. It is so tempting to get in a rut, delude ourselves that time stops just for us. Meanwhile, subtly, change is going on all around us.

And then one morning, we walk the fall garden and can see our breaths trail ahead of us. A dusting of snow melts against our upturned faces. At our feet, the ground grows hard to the point of cracking. Only stubble stands where daisies turned their faces toward the sun.

Thousands of years ago, our ancestors measured their lives by the passing of the solstice, that mysterious solar cycle. Its rhythm becomes embedded in our DNA. The human journey calls us to live in the shadow of nights that encroach on the light until they seem never to end.

We all have had such dark moments—days and weeks, even years. In the fallow garden we take hope. This, too, shall pass. The garden lives on as a monument to the spiritual necessity of patience.

Some of the most joyous holidays come amid those bleakest dates on the calendar. We deck our halls with strings of brilliant light and hang greenery on our barren doorways. Our gardening moves indoors.

One of my own favorite houseplants this time of year is not the much abused poinsettia but the so-called holiday cactus [species Schlumbergera]. I have several of them, huge and magnificent succulents, scattered around my home. Funny thing, despite all my research into their care, the crazy plants never bloom.

I took to setting them outside in summer. In fall they move indoors, to darkness that supposedly triggers their bloom cycle. I even tried covering the pots with black plastic. I wait. A 'good year' means I might spot a half dozen crimson flowers on one of them. Next year I try again, varying the conditions, hoping for a miracle.

I know what the results ought to look like. When friends say, "What incredibly healthy looking plants," I just smile. Whatever my skills as a gardener, tenacity is slowly becoming one of them.

The fantastic thing about gardens is that they are real—not about some fantasy world of eternal sunshine. And like love in that wonderful Schmidt and Jones musical, there is joy in the pursuit of our vision, even in deepest throes of winters to come.

For Everything a Season
...The Year Comes Full Circle

And so the year—and this book—come full circle. Fifty-two weeks have played themselves out in the garden, a cycle that defines the very essence of life on planet earth.

Our society needs a constant reminder of what it means to live on 'garden time'. For today's youth-obsessed culture, time becomes the enemy. Nips and tucks and botox conspire to stop time in its tracks. Not so in the garden. Without the seasonal progression of time, there can be no garden. Without the rain and fallow times, no growth. The rhythm of the seasons is nature's perpetual call to renewal. Hope springs.

The frozen world of December is not the end, but only the beginning. January thaws await. Long winter nights slowly lose their icy grip on the land. Sunlight lingers, timidly at first, its warming rays touching the depths of the most intractable snow banks. Melt water lifts a mirror to the roiling gray clouds overhead. The rising gusts of April are heavy with the promise of life-giving rain. And even in the starkest desert landscape, buds begin to form on the spiny skin of the cactus.

In the urban landscape, the engines of our imagination have learned to regulate the very air we breathe, defy summer heat and wintery blasts. That struggle to control our destiny is as old as humanity itself.

Poppies—traditional symbols of loss and remembrance—honor the beauty and fragility of life.

Laboring on behind cubicle walls, workers punch clocks that track their every minute. Sadly, too often one day becomes like any other.

Gardeners embrace another reality. In the garden, cold and drought, howling wind and rising water ultimately answer to no one—a humbling reality check. For everything its season. The turning of the year from seedtime to harvest, plowing and planting, cultivating and uprooting unfolds in familiar beauty, but also mystery.

In place of the quest for control, the gardener substitutes *mindfulness*, the humility to tread gently. It matters where things are planted. Lessons learned from past sins of overuse and wanton depletion of nature's bounty inform humankind's future. Putting back becomes a necessity, a way of life.

Even in the face of abuse, the wounded earth often proves more forgiving than humankind deserves. Come drought and fire, the scars on the land are capable of healing. Nature's tears bathe the earth, taking with it the failures of seasons past. Fallow months ensure the time to regroup and prepare for another time of growing. The relationship with the land begins afresh.

Good gardeners become masters at knowing when to rein in and when to let go, when to deadhead and when fragile shoots need to struggle skyward on their own. Books and manuals can help, but the consummate teacher is experience and the wisdom to learn from it as the seasons unfold.

At root, a gardener's pact with the earth is to love unconditionally. Tending the earth becomes a spiritual exercise in patience, hope, selfless discipline, accountability.

Then, too, successful gardening becomes all about building community. Humanity can learn a great deal from those long-established stands of perennials in the garden. The human story is driven by the urge to reach out to the 'other' wherever we are planted. The roots that ground us become a measure of our maturity. And diversity becomes the garden's best defense against the unknown. The whole-ness of the human garden becomes richer than any of its individual parts.

It is no coincidence that religious traditions envision Paradise as a garden or that encounters with the Sacred come as humankind walks in the garden in the cool of the day. No accident either that places of burial at the end of our journey's often appear cultivated like lush and flowering parklands. In the end, our destiny is to return to the garden, the dust from which life springs.

The story of our spiritual journey, like the gardener's year, comes full circle. In life's deepest losses lie the seeds of new beginnings. In the face of death, life goes on.

Yet even as a gardener wrestles with the spiritual truths that plants and a garden can teach, words seem poor substitutes for the feel of the dirt underfoot, the callouses that testify to work accomplished. All the senses—touch, taste, smell, sight and even hearing—come into play as we tend and nurture and yes, *enjoy*.

It is in that spirit I offer up these notes and thoughts on what the garden means in my own life. Shared wisdom knows no date or day or hour. The heroine in my Life in the Garden novels, garden writer Eve Brennerman, keeps a Calendar of Garden Quotations on her kitchen counter to remind her of what counts in her life. Every January or close to it, she shuffles the 365 tiny cards and lets the truth of the gardener's art speak to her afresh.

It is my hope that with time the pages of this book might come to track every readers' own journey, as favorite pages begin to open automatically to the touch without benefit of bookmarks. In an uncertain world, the familiar grounds us. But then so does that moment of surprise, the sights and insights that stop us in our tracks and help us to rethink where we are headed and why. In the garden, such vistas draw us faithfully day after day—as comforting as greatgrandma's lilac bush and as challenging as the random sprouts and shoots that cause us to rethink our well-laid plans for the garden's future.

For everything a season. *May your time in the garden be full of love and beauty. Always.*

Words like 'risk' and 'hope' and 'grace' do not pop up a lot in horticultural magazines. That is odd, because you cannot survive in the gardening business long without them. Time in a Garden, 2006.

About the Author

Author Mary Agria has won critical praise for her novels that uniquely capture the voices and choices of men and women facing retirement, loss and other challenging changes in their life journeys. After earning a Master's Degree from the University of Wisconsin-Madison, Agria spent her early career as a researcher, program director and technical writer in the field of rural development. Her syndicated newspaper column on work force issues ran for 22 years. Her gardening novel set in Northern Michigan, *TIME in a Garden*, became a regional best-seller in 2006. She followed it with a series of highly successful novels about rural life: *Vox Humana: The Human Voice*; *In Transit*; *Community of Scholars*. The sequels in her Life in the Garden series, the reviewer-acclaimed *Garden of Eve* and *From the Tender Stem* (2015) chronicle the life of garden columnist Eve Brennerman, her family and neighbors as they struggle to find meaning in their lives.

For 14 years following his retirement as President Emeritus of the University of Dubuque, Dr. John Agria served as official photographer for an internationally known summer music festival in Northern Michigan. He also collaborated with his wife on a book about that historic Michigan Chautauqua: *Bay View: Images of America*, (Arcadia Press, 2014). His photos also illustrate her children's book *Second Leaves: Growing Young Gardeners*. He has taught workshops on photography and freelanced as a photographer on Long Island. His photo restorations were featured in two major exhibitions by the Greenport, NY Historical Society.

AT RIGHT: The author makes a pilgrimage to Impressionist painter Claude Monet's garden in Giverney, France.

Channel your Inner Gardener
with these Classics from Mary A. Agria

Set in northern Michigan resort country, this 2006 best-seller begins the unforgettable saga of Eve and her crew of fellow community gardeners--celebrating perennial gardens, family and the enduring power of human love. **"A must-read for the contemplative gardener."** Suffolk Times. Five-Star judge's review, 2007 *Writer's Digest Self-Published Book Awards*, Literary Fiction. ISBN-13: 978-1411687028

A powerful chronicle of a woman's growth in the aftermath of unbearable loss. **"A tender, intelligent, heartbreaking and joyous celebration of the circle of life and the seasons."** *Award-winning garden and nature writer, Sharon Lovejoy.* ISBN 978-1-4583-6799-0.

NEW in 2015: The saga of garden writer Eve Brennerman and the unforgettable cast of characters on the community garden crew continues. Third in the Life in the Garden series, the novel is a love-song to the power of gardening to ground us, whatever the ages of stages of our lives. ISBN-978-1-312-33939-2

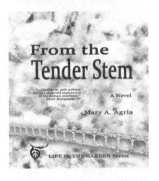

And for the young gardener in your life: **"A deft fusion of storybook, early reader and beginning botany book . . . a child's view of gardening with an adult who cares about growing and them."** *Award-winning McLean & Eakin Booksellers, Petoskey.* ISBN-13: 978-1105325090

The intriguing worlds of pipe organs and weaving come together in this poignant story of a woman facing forced retirement. **"a reflective portrayal of the ascent of goodness, reconciliation and love,"** *AGO Magazine*, 2007
ISBN-13: 978-1430317593

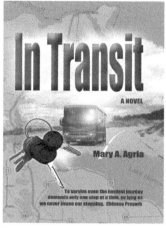

When widow Lib Aventura, a former travel agent, finds the courage to return to the U.P. and reclaim her abandoned motorhome, she discovers that her journey is only beginning. **"...wisdom, the kind that only a lifetime of experience can give. Like Lib may we never grow too old to live."** *Dan's Hamptons*, 2008
ISBN-13: 978-1435709645

An accusation of sexual harassment challenges a tiny Pennsylvania campus to rethink what it means to be an "academic community". **"Five stars, highly recommended. . . a riveting thriller of academe."** *Midwest Book Review, 2009* *ISBN-13: 978-0578015590*

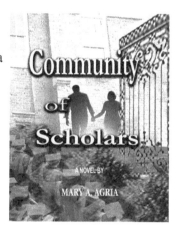

New in 2014 from Dr. John J. and Mary A. Agria...A photo history of the Michigan Chautauqua Community, Bay View. **"Melds text and images in a way that captures the uniqueness of the area and its culture".** *Arcadia Press.* ISBN-13: 978-1467111669

For sample chapters, photos and special features, visit maryagria.com